SHAW

A Biography by
Scott M. Morris

Micro-Books, Incorporated
Windermere, Florida
32786

Copyright © 1988 by Scott Morgan Morris
All rights reserved.
No part of this book may be reproduced
in any form or by any means
without the prior written permission of
Micro-Books, Inc.,
excepting brief quotes used in connection
with reviews written specifically for
inclusion in a magazine, newspaper, or
other review.
Micro-Books, Inc.
P.O. Box 457
Windermere, Florida 32786
First printing, March, 1988

CREDITS:
Verses adapted from "The Hollow Men"
in Collected Poems 1909—1962 by T. S. Eliot,
copyright © 1936 by Harcourt Brace Jovanovich, Inc.;
copyright © 1963, 1964 by T. S. Eliot.
Reprinted by permission of the publisher.
Williams New Testament, copyright © 1986,
Holman Bible Publishers.

Library of Congress Catalog Card Number 87-12410
ISBN 0-941485-04-8

Printed in the United States of America

APPRECIATIONS

At my age, it is a once in a lifetime opportunity to be asked to write a book. When I started the project I was told that the biography shouldn't exceed one hundred and twenty pages. After I began to research Walter Shaw's life I soon realized the book would require a few additional pages for clarification.

From the outset, I made some important decisions, and I think it would be helpful to share these with the reader. First – this is not a comprehensive biography. Though it has been thoroughly documented, it is by no means an academic work. Walter Thiel Shaw is not a figure of great historical importance, in any case, not now. Perhaps people need to know every detail about Napoleon's life. Not so with my subject. This is a powerful story. Each fact has been verified by Shaw and cross-referenced with newspaper articles and court records. No attempt has been made however, to determine the views of the other people that are in the biography. It is not their story. Walter has read every word. It was of grave importance to me that the truth be told, not just factually – but emotionally. And not what Walter wanted people to think he thought or felt *but what he did in fact think and feel*. I can tell you that our interviews closely resembled nightmarish inquisitions. There were many arguments and even a few tears. Yelling became commonplace. Many of the questions I ask Walter were deeply personal. They caused him pain. I wanted to peel away every layer of pretense and I hoped that what remained would be an accurate portrayal of not only the life, but more importantly, the mind of a very brutal human being.

At last the struggle has ended. The book has been written

and it is true. True as Ernest Hemingway spoke of truth in writing, that which is emotionally honest.

There are several accounts I must settle before I finish. I am indebted to many people, too many to mention.

Lisa Pettis, my typist, gets a special award of merit for heroically deciphering my handwriting.

Arthur E. Janz, who typeset, as well as assisted in the editing of this book – thanks Artie.

Scott Boman, for his invaluable help in editing the manuscript.

Appreciated greatly "Uncle" Fred's and "Aunt" Mary's advice.

My friend, Scott Jones for his humor – humor is the quintessential perspective for life. Thanks for the light perspective.

I must thank Jennifer Johnson for her undying strength and support.

Julianne, my sister, I love you.

Mom – I have been told that we are judged by our fruits. I am far from ripe, but thanks to you, I'm not rotten. I love you Mom.

Finally, to my father, who's severe and often painful critiques, combined with tenacious support, saved me again and again. What can I say Dad, I wish I were just like you – life is beautiful, when your hero is your father. I love you.

Scott Morgan Morris
April 17, 1987

DEDICATION

Anyone reading this biography will realize that the Lord has "brought me up out of a horrible pit..." (Psalm 40: 2). I owe everything to God.

The Lord saw fit to influence two ministers to have a great impact on my life. I became a Christian under the ministries of pastor Wil Cohron, and pastor Danny Drake. The latter has been my pastor and counselor. Both of these men have demonstrated God's love over and over again.

God, in His wisdom, also brought Barbara into my life. We met, fell in love, and married. She took my hand to walk with me without any realization, at first, that the best was yet to come.

I often find myself thinking of inmates who are still incarcerated. They, as I did, got off to a bad start. It's my sincere hope that many of those unfortunate men an women will read this book. The Lord can do for them what He did for me.

It is important to me to mention many people who have touched my life: Dr. E.J. Daniels, recently deceased, who believed my story should be told. (He introduced me to Scott Morris who wrote this biography.) Naturally, I wish to thank my two precious children, Randy and Michele for their understanding. They suffered because of me, but kept on loving me anyhow.

My mother and father shed barrels of tears over me. I wish my mother could have read this book. She passed away shortly before it was completed.

There also is Dr. Robert Helmer and his lovely wife Sandy as well as Mr. Algee and Annie Outlaw, Mr. Duke and Anne Dupree, Mr. Mike and Maxine Taylor and Ed Bondi along with Mr. Joseph Guise.

Mr. Scott Morris didn't tire in probing and pushing. He forced me to look way down deep as I never had before.

Last, but not least, I want to express my deepest gratitude to Mr. John Russo who was, and always will be, an enormous inspiration to me.

Senator Daniel Jenkins and his wife as well as Dr. Harold Hunter and his wife helped me unselfishly by endorsing me for the ministry. They have shown faith in me and in my quest to bring people to Christ. To all of those who have believed in me I owe undying thanks.

I have been blessed by their association.

Walter Thiel Shaw, Jr.

TO MY MOTHER

Miami, Florida was a turbulent place in 1948. Jackson Memorial Hospital was even more turbulent on January 27, when Betty Lou Roberts-Shaw checked into the maternity ward, brought in by her husband and her father.

Shortly after her admittance I saw the light of day and felt my mother's loving arms although, of course, I didn't know until many years later just how much a mother could love her son.

While I was a toddler I gave her all the pleasures a young boy could give his mother. Unfortunately, due to circumstances unexplainable to me during my years as a teenager, I must admit that while I, of course, returned her love, I failed her terribly. God, as He is in my heart today, was not then, and problems I gave her as a son were brought on by me, and me only.

My inspiration were far from being spiritual and her guidance and help were of little, if any, concern to me. Instead, I was more interested in material things. I was impressed by worldly possessions of others, and didn't care if they were ill-gotten or not. My school mates and my friends owned bicycles, they owned wristwatches, and their pockets were full of money. I, in turn, didn't have those things and in my childish way of thinking I blamed my dear mother for those shortcomings as she only supplied me with a sparse amount of money which was hardly more than the cost of the milk I bought in school and an occasional candy bar.

The Sunday walks to our church were a waste of time as far as I remember today. The sermons of our minister were dull, and I only joined the prayers to please my mother. None of my friends, those who owned their bicycles, watches, and fine shoes, didn't attend the services — I never saw them attend church with their families. I joined their activities.

There were times when I despised the warnings of my mother. Today, of course, I'm wise enough to know how right she was.

I'm terribly sorry that I gave her so much heartache and I'm sorry that she can't see me now. It's too late to say to her, "Mom, I love you." God has taken her from me too soon.

This book? She was a great part of the inspiration to let my story be told. She would have been the proudest mother on earth to see how well I have turned out to be.

It's my quest now to make up for having failed my mother. It's my desire to live the life she intended for me to live. And so, my dear Mom, please forgive me for the tears I brought to you. Now I know what you tried to do. At long last, you have succeeded.

Walter Theil Shaw, Jr.

1

CHAPTER ONE

"Those who believe, that man's good lies in the flesh, and evil in the things that induce him to turn his back on the pleasures of the senses, deserve to become glutted with them and to die of them."

Blaise Pascal

"What is at once infinitely complex and wholly predictable? – Why, man, of course."

S. Morris

RÉSUMÉ

Walter Thiel Shaw, Jr.
Date of Birth – January 27, 1948
Place of Birth – Miami, Florida

PHYSICAL DESCRIPTION
Height – 5'11"
Weight – 165 pounds
Hair – Brown

Eyes – Dark brown
Distinguishing Marks – Multiple scars on wrists, left hand, face, and abdomen

EDUCATION
High School – Miami Central High, Miami, Florida, graduate
College – Dade Junior College (one semester).
Graduate Studies – Under the special tutelage of America's leading crime bosses

MARITAL STATUS
Married 1967, Bonnie Helton (two children). Divorced 1977.
Married 1980, Marianne Duke. Divorced 1981.

PLACES OF RESIDENCE
Miami, Florida
New York, New York
Oakland, New Jersey
Fort Lauderdale Prison Annex
Arcadia County Jail
Tarpon Springs Work Release Center
North Sumter Correctional Institute
Tavares County Jail
Brevard County Correctional Institute
DeSoto Correctional Institute
Butner Federal Penitentiary, North Carolina
Lake Butler Medical Reception Center
Florida State Penitentiary (Death Row)

CAREER EXPERIENCE
1965 – Busboy and dishwasher at the International House of Pancakes, 87th Street and Biscayne Boulevard Miami,

Florida
1966 – Shoe salesman
1966 – Specialist in check, money order, and travel check forgery
1967 – Bagman for the nation's largest extortion ring
1967 – Thoroughbred racehorse owner
1968 – Soldier for national Mafia boss
1969 – "Art" collector and distributor
1969 – Member of infamous Dinner Time Burglar ring
1970 – Owner of Global Excavating, Archie's Pants, and the Apple Boutique, through extortion
1975 – Leader of the Dinner Time Burglar ring. Annual gross income $10,000,000
1967–1975 – Suspect in burglarizing the Dupont Estate, Gloria Vanderbilt's Palm Beach home, and the Liberace mansion, among others

AREAS OF EXPERTISE

Intimidation	Blackmail	Deception
Firearms	Brutality	Forgery
Burglary	Land Swindles	Extortion
Check Kiting	Fake ID's	
Counterfeiting	Death	

HOBBIES

Prostitutes	Gambling
Nightclubs	Sports Cars
Booze	Airline Stewardesses
Racetracks	Handguns

CRIMINAL RECORD
Arrests – Between 1967–1975, arrested 27 times for crimes ranging from extortion, counterfeiting, kidnapping, cocaine trafficking, burglary, grand theft, and suspicion of first –

degree murder.
First Conviction – Burglary, sentenced to 15 years, 1975.
Second Conviction – Burglary, sentenced to 15 years, 1975.
Third Conviction – Cocaine trafficking, sentenced to 12 years, 1975, federal conviction.
Fourth Conviction – Burglary, sentenced to 7 years, 1975.

REFERENCES
Archie (John) Geanunzio – Formerly the head of the nation's largest bookie organization.
Frank Sacco – Expert in extortion and leader of a far-flung extortionist's ring, one of the biggest in the world.
"The Bear" – National crime boss.
Peter Joseph Salerno – Top jewel thief. Founder and mastermind of the infamous multimillion – dollar burglary ring referred to by the media as the Dinner Time Burglars.
Anthony Grecco – High – profile Sicilian mob boss, also known by his alias, "Tom Palmer."
Annello "Little Lamb" Della Croce – Recognized as one of the nation's deadliest bosses, earned his reputation by dressing up as a priest, gun hidden in a hole cut out of a Bible, to perform "last rites" on many unfortunate victims.

RECOMMENDATIONS
– *"He ain't no sissy . . ."*
                              Bob "French" Clark,
                fellow gang member in elementary school

– *"The Crazy Kid"*
                One of America's current two top Mafia bosses

– *"A walking Who's Who of organized crime"*
                Police sources as quoted by *The Miami Herald*

– *"Top newsmaker of 1975"*
                                Hollywood Sun-Tattler

– *"Sexiest eyes of any man I've ever met . . ."*
       Marianne Duke, centerfold model and former callgirl

– *"Tell Walter I will always love him"*
           Howard Wieselberg, a homosexual destroyed
                      by Shaw through extortion

– *"The most selfish man in the world"*
                                    Bonnie Helton,
        childhood sweetheart and wife for ten years

– *"He ruled with guns and threats"*
    Gene Tyce, a member of the Dinner Time Burglar ring

"Right out of Humphrey Bogart"
    Detective Tranfa, Hallandale, Florida, Police Department

– *"He's a real pro"*
                    Detective Sergeant, Marco Cerintelli

– *"Master Criminal"*
                  Lisa Conners, *Jacksonville Times-Union*

– *"A Modern Day Jesse James"* and *"never encountered a more colorful character."*
             Federal District Judge Norman C. Roettger, Jr.

. . . *The story begins in New Jersey*

2

CHAPTER TWO

Walter Shaw, Jr., twelve years old, had been waiting in the academy lobby for thirty minutes. His father was late. As he twisted impatiently, a four-door blue Ford drove into the circular driveway that formed the academy's promenade. Walter hardly took notice of the vehicle. His father always traveled in a black chauffeur-driven limousine. It was the limousine that he looked for.

Two men made their way to the lobby. The men, both of medium height and build, opened the lobby doors and took off their sunglasses. One of the men managed a smile when he saw the boy and asked if he wasn't Walter Shaw's son. "We're trying to locate your dad on some business," one explained. "We're old friends," added the other.

Walter stated that his father was a busy man and it was not surprising that they could not find him, but if they needed to see him, "Dad's suppose to be here now to pick me up."

The men smiled politely and left. Walter watched them from the lobby. They *must* be old friends, he reasoned. They talked, dressed, and looked different from his father's recent companions. These men were the very essence of plainness – not too tall or short, medium build, no definite accents, not a hint of charm. They were dull and they furthered their unflattering impression as they sat motionless in their car.

Walter rocked in his chair, grew angry, and finally, his energy dissipating, he yawned. Then his half-closed, lazy eyes spotted the approaching Lincoln Continental limousine.

The monotonous morning had left him unprepared for the next few minutes. The chauffeur spotted the two occupants of the blue Ford and pushed Walter's` father into the backseat, slamming the gas pedal to the floor. The black Continental activated all eight cylinders and the tires spun feverishly. The men in the Ford frantically started their car in pursuit. Soon the race had passed beyond Walter's line of vision.

The two men were chasing the limousine, which meant that his father was in trouble. One thing was certain, the two men had lied about being old friends.

He sat quietly. The deadness of early afternoon crept back. The promenade was empty. The lobby was empty. Now everything was still. Weary, he walked to his room and fell upon his bunk. A tear forced its way through one of his tightly closed eyes. Something had gone wrong.

• • • • •

A hand prodded his shoulder. The tears had dried and left his eyes and face crusty. He could not determine if he had been asleep for minutes or hours, although it seemed as though he had been out for a while. Feeling used and worn – out, he lay upon his bed like a lump of trash ready to be thrown away. And he remembered – before he was even conscious of being awake his mind was scorched with the realization that what had taken place earlier was not a dream. The hand continued pressing for a reaction.

"I'm awake," he said blankly.

It was Mr. Sarcka, the headmaster of the academy. For the first time, he looked compassionate. He told Walter to pack his things and go to the infirmary. "At nine o'clock your mother will call you," he continued.

Something warm at last. He could talk to his mother. She would know what was going on.

After packing his clothes and personal items into a metal chest, he dragged it behind him and rounded the corner to the infirmary. Headmaster Sarcka unlocked the infirmary door, invited Walter in, flicked the light switch, and shut the door before passing to the back of the small room.

"What's happened to Dad?" Walter asked. Headmaster Sarcka looked into his eyes weakly. "Your mother will talk with you, tonight." Sarcka avoided the question. Walter just turned away. He neither expected nor wanted an answer from the headmaster.

Next Sarcka clasped his hands together and offered some rather redundant instructions. "There's the cot if you're tired, and on the counter you'll find some plastic cups. So if you want something to drink – of course, you can turn the lights off or leave them on to read. I, well anyway, I will return for you when your mother calls," he said, and left.

The sound of shoes smacking the floor reverberated down the corridor. Alone now, Walter sank down into the middle of the cot and rested his back against the wall. The room was sterile, cold, and quiet. It was unbearably orderly and within its walls not one distracting object resided. There wasn't a window. Nor was there a magazine to page through.

He began to drift in and out of a restless sleep. His nerves were exhausted from maintaining a steady intensity, but they would not bend. Fevered, now and again he would press his cool palm against his brow to relieve a throbbing pain. He had never really had a headache before. His body, it seemed, was strangely disjointed from his head. He was existing beyond his body. Conscious only of the inferno within his skull, his body was cold and far away.

Suddenly there were voices outside his door. The dialogue was hushed but furious. "I told you Shaw's dad was a gangster – how else would the big shot have known so much?"

"You're full of it; you believed him too."

"Did not."

"Shut up, just slide the paper under the door – whatever you believe, *The New York Times* don't lie."

The whispering ceased as someone slid a newspaper under the infirmary door; a stampede of running feet and laughter followed. The assassins were elated, they had killed a giant and now they could choose a new king. Adolescent boys do not make loyal subjects.

Walter gazed at the paper. Something in it carried a concluding significance for the eventful day. Rolling his eyes, he cursed the room. He cursed his fever and the throbbing, and turned his body to the back of the room and stared at the long neck of the faucet. He noticed the locks on each cabinet door, trying to study anything except the rumpled paper on the floor.

Unfolding himself from the cot he walked to the door and reached for the paper. His heart began to pump faster. A turbulent heat swept across his chest and settled in his stomach. When he finished reading the pencil circled copy he gasped. His heart had lodged itself in his throat and now it was swelling and driving a painful beat. Looking frantically around the small room, he sought an accuser or someone to accuse. His own heart was entangling his vocal chords, leaving him with silence. And there in black print, in *The New York Times,* was his father's name.

His father, the article said, was connected with the Mafia ... had been arrested and placed in jail ... was a member of the

Mafia . . . a criminal. A criminal. The word ripped his guts like exploding shrapnel. At last Walter freed his lungs with a deafening scream.

Sobbing, he gulped in oxygen to feed his grief. He stood until he could cry no more, let the paper drop to his feet, and kicked it under the cot. The humiliation of the afternoon burned his temples. After turning the lights out, he settled on the cot face up. The last bit of water left his eyes as he looked up at the ceiling. He was unable to focus his eyes and gazed at no particular part of it. Staring into the darkness, with its peaceful consistency, lulled him into a trance, and his trance gave way to sleep — a jerky, dreamless sleep.

A light flooded the room and startled him. He twisted his head around to see the headmaster standing in the doorway. "Your mother is on the phone," he said.

The headmaster took him out of the building into the night air. Rubbing his arms for warmth, Walter walked into the headmaster's quarters.

"She's on now," the headmaster said, pointing to the telephone.

His mother spoke calmly and a smile cracked the glaze that covered Walter's cheeks. It was his first smile all day. He was going home.

The return trip was by bus. During the ride he thought of his mother. After six months at military academy he looked forward to the material and emotional benefits of his family, but when the bus arrived, a change swept over him. He felt queasy. Something was floating about his head loose, something that was a part of his mind, and yet free from the mass of brain tissue. It was a thought, a thought of horrible consequences, and he fought it. He tried to smile as he walked into the terminal, but he was losing the mental battle. There stood his mother. He went blank. As she ran to him he opened his mouth to say, "I love you," but "What's happened to Dad?" burst forth angrily instead. As his mother reached for his hand, he jerked it away. "Did you see what the paper said about him?" he asked.

He could not stand the idea of someone touching his skin. Then he turned away from his mother and in an instant it overcame him. The woeful realization, the terrible possibility, that had been menacingly circling his skull, suddenly clawed into his consciousness and embedded itself: He was not home... only somewhere *else*. He turned back. His mother looked like a strange, broken little woman. She was almost unrecognizable. He did not want to go back or forward. His skin cracked with heat and he was embarrassed. Surely people were watching him sink.

Yes, he thought, he *was* sinking, or perhaps disappearing. The scene grew sickening. The thoughts now vibrating in his flesh were rushing signals throughout his body. He understood. There was no pretending, nor was this a phase. At twelve years old he was completely *alone*.

On the way home there was little conversation. His mother drove slowly, trying to hold back the tears. Her son frightened her, and she did not have good news for him.

Finally she answered the question he had been afraid to ask. "Your father got mixed up with that filthy man you call your uncle. He's innocent, but the government doesn't know that, the way he kept meeting with him. You can't trust people, period. But your father won't listen and now he finds out the hard way."

In the weeks that followed, the maid and gardener were dismissed. The Thunderbird and Cadillac were sold, and movers transported furniture from their Miami Shores home to a unpretentious house in Ives Estate, on the other side of Miami.

3

CHAPTER THREE

Archie John Geanunzio was the nation's largest bookie. He was also the financial backer for Walter's father.

Before Walter had enrolled in Oakland Military Academy, he came to look upon Archie Geanunzio as a hero. Uncle Archie, he called him. Geanunzio, in turn, pampered the youth with money, crime stories, and on one occasion a pint-sized trench coat.

Uncle Archie stood five feet nine inches. At one hundred ninety pounds he was a good deal overweight. He dressed meticulously. Each silk tie looked as if it had been carved onto his collar. Pockmarked and pale, the skin on his face accentuated his blazing eyes. Walter was convinced there could be no loftier achievement than to succeed in emulating Uncle Archie.

Betty Lou, Walter's mother, balked, demanding that her son be removed from Archie's degrading sphere of influence. She was raised by devout Plymouth brethren, and for her hard work was a code of honor and integrity. Beautiful, this Olivia de Havilland look – alike ignored her husband's role in the

Mafia, but she refused to sit idle while her son's mind was being molded by sinister forces. She reeled when Walter sported his miniature black trench coat. "Look what's happening to your son," she said to her husband, "today a trench coat, tomorrow a shotgun."

Walter was sent away but his father continued to do business with the aging mafioso.

In 1959 Walter's father, already well-known as an electronic's genius, created a telephonic breakthrough dubbed the black box. The black box was a portable unit that allowed toll-free long-distance telephone calls, and rendered a phone line untappable. Geanunzio and associates were flushed with enthusiasm, but their excitement never came to fruition. Their plans spoiled when Joe Valachi, a member of the secret crime organization La Cosa Nostra, turned over and leaked their names to hungry FBI investigators. The charge against Walter Sr. was unlawfully attaching a device to a Bell Telephone line. Next he received a subpoena to appear before the United States Senate's McClellan Subcommittee on Improper Activities in the Labor and Management Fields.

To retaliate against the subpoena, Walter's mother ran about the house screaming that there was "Mafia hysteria" because of the activities of Chief Counsel Bobby Kennedy. She justified the situation to her son by adding that the government was conducting a witch hunt in Washington and "unfortunately your father's trusting people put him at the wrong place at the wrong time."

Nothing that surrounded Walter was familiar. The small house in Ives Estates was a demeaning step down from their Miami Shores home. His two sisters gave him no comfort either. One was much older, and his baby sister, Crystal, did not fulfill the necessary requirement of companionship – verbal communication. The thought of his father being in a prison in New York was unfathomable. He had concluded that his dad was simply incapable of any illegal activities. When his faith ebbed, he referred to Uncle Archie's famous maxim: "The only difference between the cops and lawyers and politicians and all the others and your Uncle Archie is that they have a license to steal."

Walter was confused but not chaotic. His mind stuck in freeze frames. He was the boy from nowhere. His mother and father were concepts. Underneath the word "Father" hung a banner that read: "innocent." His mind worked like that. There were no details, systematic thinking, or conclusions – only concepts.

When he enrolled in Ives Estates Elementary School, he was determined not to learn anything. Weary of activities and information, he was preoccupied with a rather poorly developed notion that philosophers might call the big picture. His big picture was so out of focus that a more accurate term would be collage. The big collage consisted of a mind's-eye view of faces and places – Uncle Archie, Oakland Military Academy, his mother, New York, and his father.

The collage had one unifying element. It represented all that was familiar to him. The central theme around which this hodgepodge of consciousness revolved was the most wrenching concept of all – betrayal. Uncle Archie and especially his mother and father, had all been betrayed. The collage was a collection of victims. Who, then, was responsible for the damage? Who had caused Uncle Archie to be arrested? Who had persuaded his friends to turn on him at Oakland? Who had forced his mother to sell her beautiful estate and move into a run-down house, and who was trying to put his father behind bars? What created the humiliation, shame, and isolation with which he lived? He deduced that the premier director in this theater of pain was Chief Counsel Bobby Kennedy.

He had never seen a picture of Bobby Kennedy, but he imagined him to be obese and unkempt – a sweaty, small-eyed man with an enormous bald head. If Bobby Kennedy were to blame, that meant the government was equally at fault, all of which seemed quite logical to a student of the Archie Geanunzio School of Reason and Ethics. There was more. If the government was corrupt, then everyone who supported it was guilty as well: the teacher who stood before him, peers surrounding him, the grocery store owner down the street. In fact, anyone who was not pictured in the collage could be designated as an enemy. His mother had warned him not to trust anyone, but never did he suspect the conspiracy to be so comprehensive. He did not come to this conclusion in one sitting. The revelation emerged slowly. For many days he could only toy with the essential conglomeration of emotions, concepts, and faces. Then, spurned by his new environment, he pursued his thesis bit by bit. The proof of his dramatic conclusion erupted in a rather physical way for the dejected philosopher.

Ives Estates Elementary School was home to a motley gang of hard-heads who roamed its corridors in search of the innocent and weak. They had learned by the sixth grade what takes some presidents and kings years of political experience to understand. It is better to be feared than loved. Russel Kane, Bob "French" Clark, and Gary Butts were three of the most powerful members. One morning during recess French confronted Walter. The gang circled around the two to insure privacy. Walter, dwarfed by the larger boys, stood firm. The words that rolled out of French Clark's mouth served as the final piece of evidence necessary for Walter to be able to state, with full academic backing, that indeed the entire world had joined hands in a dastardly attempt to destroy himself, Uncle Archie, his mother, and his father.

French taunted, "I hear your dad's a gangster."

Walter considered French's jeering remark an invitation for demonstrative debate. He entered his rebuttal with an eloquent looping left hook which clipped French's nose. By the time French reached for his face, blood had already begun to pour steadily from each nostril. He tried to stop the flow. It was no use. He clenched his fists and eyed his opponent. Walter peered at French, disbelieving. French did not appear to be in pain. Rather, he looked like an angry bull that had been pushed far beyond its limit. Walter knew then that there would be no cross-examination. French drew his clublike arms into a fighting position and proceeded to parlay a series of jabs that would settle any forensic contest. When Walter could stand the pain no longer, his legs buckled under him compassionately, and he slumped to the ground. The hungry crowd satiated, French ordered his highly disciplined squad to disperse, leaving Walter to collect his pride which had been scattered about the schoolyard.

Walter sat motionless without a single thought for several minutes. The numbness gave way to sharp pains, and with the pain, he began to think again. His body was battered and his face was swelling like a balloon. He felt like an ill-shaped cask, hollow, but warped and stiff outside. When the bell rang, ending the morning break, he picked himself up and walked home.

The instant his mother saw him she gave way to hysteria, moaning and uttering half-phrases. Walter wanted to push her away and sit alone in his room, but her maternal instincts would not be denied. He had endured a good beating, surely he could withstand his mother's torturous medical practices. She examined, doctored, had him repeat the events that had unfolded into the bloodbath, over and over again and finally permitted him to go to his room. After submitting to the half-hour healing ritual, he was exhausted. He collapsed on his small bed.

The next morning he could barely see out of his left eye and his right eye provided only a marginal improvement. His cheeks were puffy and his body ached. He marveled that he could have been beaten so thoroughly. Worse, he could think of no sound way to prevent a similar situation from occurring again. When he returned to school, as anticipated he was confronted by French. Surrounded by enthusiastic thrill-seekers, Walter eyed French. He knew he could cower and beg for pardon, but he would not. French was not just a sixth-grade bully. He was an antagonist directed through a long chain of sinister people who found their sole source of authority in Bobby Kennedy. Walter would not bow to the same evil people who were punishing his father.

"What do you want?" Walter asked.

French stuck his hand out, hubris seething from his body.

"We decided to let you in the gang because you took your beating like a man . . . He ain't no sissy," French shouted to the onlookers.

Walter had misjudged his opponent. This was no Bobby Kennedy man, this was an individualist right out of the mold of Uncle Archie. With French and his gang, the potential for decisive action against the system was enormous. Alone, he could accomplish little. With a gang including the likes of Russel Kane, Gary Butts, and of course, French Clark, he could wreak havoc. He burned with a passion to destroy something, anything, everyone, maybe the whole world. Corrupt and canker-infested, the world deserved brutality. His fearlessness and zeal for attention soon placed him in a leadership role with the gang.

By the time Walter entered junior high, just thirteen years old, his loyal troops had become quite boisterous. The group stayed out until eleven or twelve every night, roaming the neighborhood. Eventually they found it easier to pass the long nights with alcoholic beverages. Passersby would gawk at the young boys in their adolescent debauchery, hooting, hollering, and openly consuming beer. After long evenings of drinking, it was necessary to skip school. Countless schooldays were passed at an ice cream store adjacent to the 7-Eleven on Ives Dairy Road. Walter performed feats of bravery at the old parlor. Smaller than his companions, he compensated for his size with bravado and daring. He sauntered into the ice cream shop, walked to the back freezer, turned, and smiled at his admirers before filling his denim jacket with Popsicles and ice cream. Still unsatisfied with his performance, he would, jacket bulging, walk up to the counter and antagonize the elderly woman tending the parlor. "Do you see any ice cream on me?" he asked. Frightened, the woman denied that she had witnessed anything. Walter laughed brazenly and strutted out of the store to share his spoils.

His mother tried to tighten the reins on him. Without a father to provide stern support, her warnings were amusing at best.

Over a year had passed since he had landed in Miami. He no longer consciously operated under the auspices of retribution. His collage of victims had given way to the more vivid realities of girls, parties, and the gang itself. He was hurting, but the pain was no longer direct. It was vague and dull. He did not enjoy seeing his mother without a husband alone in a project-style home in Ives Estates. Money was scarce and boredom was plentiful. Without an expensive anesthesia to deaden the grinding insecurity, a loneliness engulfed him, and he continued his retaliation. When one is hurting, one either heals or hurts back. Walter was not healing.

He had asked his mother for a bicycle. She responded that there wasn't enough money for one, but if there were, she still would not purchase a bike until he improved his grades and discontinued his roguish behavior. Walter assured her that he would have a bicycle by Christmas without her help.

Bored with the popsicle raids, Walter gathered his cohorts about him for a secret meeting to plan his first overt criminal act. It was decided that he and Gary Butts would steal a brand-new red Schwinn bicycle from a boy in Ives Estates. They staked out the house, and one evening after midnight, Gary forced the garage door open. Walter scrambled inside, grabbed the bike, and he and Gary, sharing the transportation, pedaled to safety. Their destination was Russel's house. The handlebars were removed and replaced by a less conspicuous pair. Russell furnished a metallic blue paint and after several hours of painstaking labor the boys agreed that the bicycle had been professionally altered and was unrecognizable. The plan might have succeeded had it not been for Danny Cooper. Danny, who fashioned himself a teenage district attorney, put an end to Walter's crime-ring by tipping off the parents of the boy whose bike had been lifted. An older brother took the case from that point. He went over to Walter's house and asked him to show him his new bike. Walter was proud of the cover-up job. Here was an opportunity to mock the boy's brother. Walter brought the bike out and rode it. This short spree was his undoing. The bike was defective; the chain skipped, and the boy's family had already discussed returning the bike to the Schwinn factory. The bicycle Walter rode, even with blue paint and new handlebars, had that unmistakable skip.

Later that evening, the blue and red lights of a police car

flashed through Walter's living room window. As his mother answered the door, he sat in his room unsure of what to do. Should he stay in his room, escape through the window, deny all accusations, what? He remembered Uncle Archie's advice and chose to follow it faithfully: "Remain cool, calm and collected. Don't let no one see you're upset."

His mother learned the details of the story and began to cry. "Walter is a good boy, he is, you know. It's just that his father is gone. It's hard on him now, no man around the house."

The officers quieted her and explained that they had come to reclaim the bike and perhaps instill a healthy fear for the law in her son. She agreed wholeheartedly. "Yes, you're kind, that's all he needs. A little discipline. He's such a smart boy . . ."

Walter walked in. One of the officers began a long solemn lecture. At the beginning of the lecture Walter looked away with an arrogant scowl, but after the officer had outlined, in detail, life inside a juvenile corrections institute, Walter followed his lips respectfully. At the conclusion of the meeting Walter's eyes were glassy. He did not admit that he was wrong, merely outnumbered, and decided that the only rational course was to remain silent and wait for a better day.

When Walter awoke the next morning, his father was seated on the edge of his bed. He hadn't seen him for two years. Dodging an arrest warrant in Florida made a visit dangerous, but something had to be done about his son. The reunion was bittersweet. His father had always been a calm man who opted for rational discussions instead of violent confrontations, but Walter had grown to view rational discussions as cowardice and violence as heroism. He was unsure as to how he should respond to his father. This was his flesh-and-blood father, not the conceptual creation to which he had sworn allegiance; a human being who could make mistakes, not just a deity victimized by a jealous world. The same frustration that had gripped him when he had first arrived in Miami now closed in again. The inner conflict hinged on two interpretations of reality, each diametrically opposed to the other. Either the world was guilty of injustice and therefore his criminal activities were justified, or his father had made a mistake and therefore his retaliatory measures were unjustified. Walter Sr. broke the silence with a loud sigh followed by a series of penetrating questions.

Walter's response was an equally searing set of questions. He asked his father if the papers were correct in associating him with the Mafia, asked if he were inventing illegal communication devices, and, at last, his tone overflowing into biting sarcasm, he asked how he could even think of approaching him if the very source of his income was illegal. His father interrupted, "You can justify the trashy things you've been doing by painting me as an evil man if you want to, but the decision is yours, you have not been *forced* into anything. You're young, but you're not stupid. Things haven't been easy for you, but look at your mother. Is she out robbing grocery stores for food?"

At that moment Walter did not care where his mother was or what she had been doing. He only wished to be alone. His father looked at him for a response. Walter was silent. Walter Sr. lifted himself from the bed and ordered his son to pack. "You're leaving with me for Washington tomorrow."

4

CHAPTER FOUR

Before he could digest the noon snack on the Washington-bound airplane, Walter was walking the beveled marble steps that led to the United States Senate. His father had taken him to Washington hoping that he might catch "Potomac Fever," replacing his criminal aspirations with dreams of becoming a senator. Washington was impressive. And the power that emanated from the Capitol building and its confident inhabitants was inspiring. But nothing could have excited Walter more than seeing Uncle Archie once again. Uncle Archie did his best to repair the fragmented relationship between Walter and his father, but he only succeeded in glorifying crime. He presented Walter with a series of doubtful explanations to prove his father's innocence. These were the stories Walter wanted to hear. "The government is jealous of us, kid, because we're Italian. We're empire builders. See, they know that, and it scares 'em, and that's why they try to lock us up."

The conspiracy theory that Walter had developed was supported by Uncle Archie, and in Walter's mind, a higher authority did not exist. He reproached himself for having doubted its validity and his father's innocence.

By the end of his stay in Washington, Walter was paying little attention to the headline-grabbing lawmakers of the McClellan Subcommittee. The historic meetings were unimportant to him. Rather, he was fascinated by lawbreakers. The smooth mafiosos held him captive. In a single day he met three of organized crime's biggest bosses. Joseph Bonanno, the titan head of New York's Bonanno family, had patted his shoulder. Vito Genovese, of New York's Genovese family, had playfully tugged his cheek and Carlo Gambino, who later became the infamous godfather or boss of the bosses, had been on hand to greet him as well.

Walter Sr. was too busy fighting for his own life to shelter his son from the charming mobsters. Huge gaps in his testimony were filled with the Fifth Amendment. He took the fifth an astounding thirty-six times. The atmosphere was tense. Under specific orders to keep himself and what he said in a low profile, he carefully wove his testimony. The Mafia was predisposed to permanently silence those who squealed.

After several weeks of grilling Walter Sr. was dismissed, decimated by the ordeal. Unable to think clearly, and thoroughly exhausted, he required rest, but there was no time to relax. Linda, his daughter, was getting married. Walter Shaw, Sr., a traditional family patriarch, viewed marriage as a sacred event. He insisted that his daughter's marriage not take place until he was there to give her away, and to give the ceremony his blessing. Unfortunately, Florida authorities were holding a warrant for his arrest for the illegal attachment of a device to a Bell Telephone line. Although the charge was unfounded, he had neither the money nor the inclination to return to the courtroom after the grueling cross-examinations before the senate committee. While in Washington, he had been warned by Geanunzio that if he were arrested in Florida, nothing could be done for him. Faced with the possibility of either missing his daughter's wedding or going to prison, he chose the lesser of two evils and booked a flight back to Miami.

The wedding was conducted quietly. After the ceremony he devised a plan enabling him to stay with his family for a few weeks before returning to New York. He secured a small house directly behind the family home to use as a hideout. Without furniture the house appeared uninhabited.

Walter Sr. emphatically warned his son to never reveal his whereabouts, explaining that the police were looking for him and that if they found him it would mean prison. Walter locked onto his father's commission like a proud pit bull, promising never to open his mouth. For days he imagined the police vigorously questioning, then cross-examining him, and he, victoriously, thwarting their drive for information. But the uniformed officers never showed.

Walter answered the door of the family home. Two men dressed in business suits presented themselves as friends of Archie Geanunzio. Walter, following his father's strict orders not to reveal his whereabouts, stated that his father wasn't there. The men insisted that it was urgent. They had to speak to Walter Sr. and, of course, they were there as emissaries of Mr. Geanunzio. The very mention of Geanunzio's name clouded Walter's head. If the men knew Uncle Archie, they were exceptions to his father's instructions, he reasoned, before leading them around to the other house. When Walter Shaw Sr.. appeared, the men informed him that they were from the Dade County Sheriff's Department and had come with a warrant for his arrest.

Walter was dumbfounded. The men did not wear uniforms; worse, they had lied. How could they have known about Uncle Archie? How could the police trick him? It was unfair. As his dad was handcuffed and led around to the front of the house, Walter cried uncontrollably and bellowed incoherent apologies. His father had little time to bandage his son's heart. He told him to settle down and call Archie in New York. Walter rushed inside and grabbed the phone to place the call. The first three times he called, Archie answered and hung up. The fourth call elicited a minor chord of compassion from the nation's leading bookie. Archie Geanunzio told Walter he was sorry. He had warned his father not to return, and there was nothing he could do to help him. After a pause, Archie placed the receiver down. Walter continued to hold the silent phone to his ear, finally examining it, turning it from side to side, and tucking it back in its cradle. There was no one to call. He had caused his father's arrest. Nothing short of freeing him could make amends.

When his mother pulled into the driveway from the grocery store, Walter expected upheaval. Instead, she listened to him and then called her father to relate the details of the arrest. He offered to make bond. The bond posted, Walter Sr. returned to the house and assured Walter that he was not to blame. He did not want him to assume a burden that was not prepared for him. After releasing his son from his nervous grip, he clumsily uttered, "I love you."

Juxtaposed emotions nearly incapacitated Walter. For months he had struggled with the possibility of his father's guilt. Then in Washington Uncle Archie had convinced him that his father was innocent, but the entire discussion was analyzed in reference to his conceptual father. Seeing his father arrested, seeing him cuffed and hauled to jail, fueled a passion for revenge, regardless of innocence or guilt. It did not, however, restore faith. No longer was it a matter of his father's culpability or the lack of it. It was a matter of deflowered fatherhood, the abasement of the image of fatherhood. The system had effaced this image, and that violation stood beyond innocence or guilt. Archie's brief conversation with him on the phone was all the more alienating. Walter was isolated, alone; and yet, he was compelled to avenge a father toward whom he felt a growing resentment.

5

CHAPTER FIVE

The next few years were consumed with a nightmare of legal battles. The Florida case against his father was based on evidence collected by Dade County State Attorney Richard Gerstein. In 1959, when Walter was enrolled in Oakland Military Academy, a friend of his father's, Ralph Satterfield had taken a black box to Miami.

Next, Satterfield, a young playboy millionaire, ran an ad in the *Miami Herald* which promised free longdistance telephone calls. The promise of the ad, illegal on its face, prompted Gerstein to conduct an investigation. He sent his chief investigator, Arthur Hutto, to follow up on the *Herald* advertisement. Hutto ordered five hundred units. Naively assuming that Hutto was a legitimate customer, the entrepreneur called Walter Sr. in New York to announce his marketing coup. Walter Sr. refused to send the units, but Satterfield persisted. He persuaded Walter Sr. to fly to Miami to meet the buyer.

In Miami, Arthur Hutto asked Walter Sr. to hook up the black box to demonstrate its capability. He was uneasy, instinctively recognizing that something was awry. After several long minutes, he told Hutto that the attachment procedures were simple and, if he was interested in the product, he could follow them himself. Hutto left. Merely inventing a potentially illegal device was not, as Walter Sr. knew, a criminal offense. The law would be broken only when the device was attached to a Bell Telephone line.

According to Walter, Gerstein had another view of the law. This view held that Shaw's presence in the room was commensurate with attaching the unit. He filed official charges and received a warrant for Shaw's arrest. The case became infinitely complex. Bell Telephone, Walter believes, had a keen interest in the black box and injected itself into the legal proceedings. Walter Sr. was in over his head. He needed the best legal service available. An attorney named Harvey St. Jean prided himself on being both expensive and expedient. Without time to argue about fees, Walter Sr. raised the money for the retainer and soon learned that St. Jean was, as promised, expensive, but hardly loyal. Listless during the trial, St. Jean questioned witnesses indifferently, and addressed the jury at half-speed. The jury returned a verdict of guilty of a misdemeanor. Sentencing would come later at the hands of Circuit Judge Jack Falk. St. Jean assured Walter Sr. that since he did not have any prior convictions, Judge Falk at most, would give him a stern lecture and a suspended sentence. What Walter Sr. did not realize was that St. Jean was available to the highest bidder. As Walter remembers hearing it, in Judge Falk's closed chambers with Gerstein, his assistant Ellen Marfonias, and Bell Telephone representatives, St. Jean agreed to withdraw from the case.

Ellen Marfonias left the "closed" conference, Walter Sr. recalls, feeling that she had been cheapened. Her husband happened to be Walter Sr.'s close friend. Walter Sr. stated that she warned him that he was being set up and recused herself from the case. In spite of the notice, Walter Sr. was unable to extricate himself. He had already exhausted his ability to raise money. St. Jean had squeezed him dry. He had gambled and lost.

On the morning of the sentence hearing, St. Jean demanded an additional fee of $5,000. Either Walter Sr. would produce the money by noon, or St. Jean would request permission to withdraw.

Walter Sr. asked him to reconsider, promised the $5,000, and pleaded for more time to put the money together. St. Jean refused. At twelve noon he requested from Judge Falk a release from the case because of his client's inability to pay reasonable fees. Falk, according to Walter Jr., acted injudiciously, granting St. Jean's request and in the next breath assigning a public defender, who in turn requested a continuance in order to prepare a presentation for his new client. Judge Falk denied the request, and at 12:45 Walter Sr. was called into a private conference. As Walter relates it, Judge Falk advised Walter Sr. that he would grant him the most lenient of sentences if he would divulge the mechanizations of the black box. Gerstein nodded his approval and a high level representative of Bell Laboratory anxiously awaited Shaw's reply. His reply was swift. He would not yield the secret of the Black Box under any circumstances. Refusing to cooperate, the sentence hearing was reconvened. In a surgical stroke Judge Falk sentenced Walter Shaw, Sr., to one of the longest jail terms in the annals of Dade County justice for such an offense. Usually, a firsttime offender in such a case was "slapped on the wrist," sentenced and given probation. Walter Shaw, Sr., was hit with thirteen months of hard jail time.

Standing immobile before Judge Falk, he found it difficult to fathom the import of the sentence. It was so unexpected, harsh, and unfair. A disciplined man, Shaw ordered the tears pushing toward his eyes to stop. They refused. Shaw was broken. He wailed out, and could not even hear the lamenting cries of his wife nearby.

Seventeen-year-old Walter surveyed the courtroom with glassy eyes. There in the back, near a corner, sat Harvey St. Jean – the man who had betrayed his father. St. Jean's face was remorseless. Walter would never forget his carnivorous stare.

Five years later Harvey St. Jean had probably forgotten the odd drama in the courtroom. It is likely that his mind had categorized it as unimportant information and shuffled it far back into files only maintained by the subconscious. Then, one balmy night, Harvey St. Jean eased his elegant Cadillac Eldorado into the parking lot of Miami Beach's famous Lincoln Mall, regularly visited by tourists from around the world. The luxury automobile, one of the fruits of his labors, glistened, making the moonlit night all the more attractive. St. Jean opened the door and pulled himself out of the car. He probably locked it just in case vandals made a parking-lot sweep. As he turned towards the mall he certainly heard the click of a shotgun perhaps followed by a calm voice and a message, the contents of which are lost to eternity. The ringing crack of a shot-gun blast stopped happy shoppers in their tracks. He grabbed the gaping hole that had been excavated from his midsection and slumped to the pavement. Harvey St. Jean was no more.

Later that night Walter Thiel Shaw, Jr., was paid a visit by two homicide detectives from the Miami Beach Police Department. The street had it that he had threatened St. Jean in the Dade County Court Building. The threats made him a suspect for first-degree murder. On top of the threat there were two other incriminating bits of information. Gene Tyce, one of Walter's partners in a series of burglaries, had been arrested, and to save his own skin he became an informant. He described an event that had occurred a few weeks before the murder. While visiting Walter's home, two men arrived with an attaché case stuffed with $50,000 in cash. The cash, Tyce said, was to seal a murder contract. Tyce had not, he allowed, heard the name of the victim. The final bit of indirect incrimination concerned the testimony of those who were some distance away in the parking lot when the gun went off. They saw a dark Continental speeding away. Walter owned a diamond-blue Continental. After grilling Walter about his activities over the last several hours, the homicide detectives concluded that they lacked sufficient evidence to bring Shaw to court. The detectives left Walter's house as Harvey St. Jean's body was being prepared at the morgue. As of 1988 the case is still unsolved.

6

CHAPTER SIX

Walter entered the eleventh grade after the hot summer that had culminated in his father's imprisonment. While most eleventh-graders were watching or participating in the festivities of fall and football games, he was working as a dishwasher and busboy at the International House of Pancakes on 87th Street and Biscayne Boulevard.

He treated his classes as detention centers and homework assignments were ignored. Unconcerned over the barrage of school notices that warned of failing grades, he sat motionless in his classes.

Each morning his mother picked him up from school and deposited him at work before going on to her job. In the evenings he walked home. The late-night half-mile walks were not therapeutic. Thoughts and plans for hurting and inflicting pain upon those who had injured his family occupied his mind. At school he maintained a solemn presence. Time and again he rehearsed the revenge he would someday carry out against those responsible for his father's betrayal. But instinctively he knew it was a time to wait. He separated himself from the wild living and petty crimes of his former friends and obediently went from school to work to bed, and back to school again.

Geanunzio had called him once. He commiserated with Walter over his father's imprisonment as best he could. He explained that things were tough for everyone and that he himself was going to serve three years in jail for tax evasion. Walter wished him luck.

With his father and Uncle Archie away, and a family to help support, Walter called a moratorium on all of his personal plans for the future. His grandmother pleaded with him to visit his father, but the best he could manage was to drive her to the jail and wait for her in the parking lot. His father hoped that at least he might visit him during work hours. Though his nights were spent behind bars, he was allowed outside of the jail on a work release program five days a week. Walter never bothered to find out where his father was working.

His lax attitude was directed toward his mother as well. His home had become a boarding house, and he was nothing more than one of the boarders. Most of his time was occupied in the weary routine of busing tables and washing dishes. Occasionally, after work, he would venture out until sunrise, leaving his eyes bloodshot and his mother's nerves frazzled. She had lost any semblance of authority over him.

Failing grades for the entire school term necessitated summer school. The summer of 1966 brought the added responsibility of caring for his grandmother. She was being eaten by a greedy cancer. Weak, her life sinking fast, Walter moved into her small house to help her with daily activities. He harbored no resentment over the assignment, even though she constantly chided him for refusing to visit his father. Overall, she had always been kind to him. He wanted to make her as comfortable as possible.

His life continued to be a tribute to lethargy. He resigned

himself to passing his summer-school classes – nothing more. Then, in what seemed a split second, his comatose existence abruptly ended. He confronted that age-old catalyst for morose young men: a beautiful young lady.

Bonnie Helton was sixteen. An A student, she decided to attend summer school to better prepare for her senior year. Although only a teenager, her beauty was known throughout Miami. She had been chosen as Key Club Sweetheart of the Year and had won the Miss Miami Central Beauty Pageant.

She was more than attractive, she was striking. Her half Cherokee Indian blood accounted for her dark skin and eyes, and her vivacious innocence ignited many amorous fires at Miami Central High School. She was not wealthy, but her beauty and intelligence had earned her the right to practice the coveted art of snobbery. Her perfect figure was only rivaled by the loveliness of her face. In short, she was a devastating influence on the male gender. Walter sat across from her in class, complimenting her with an irresistible urge to let his eyes drift from the lecture board to her side of the room. There, in the classroom, his desire to avenge his father and blacken the world with terror died in a crossfire of love. Bonnie Helton became his present and his future. The past could hardly be remembered. Eventually, the lovesick stupor and timid glances gave way to a fervent courtship.

Initially, his love was of the unrequited variety. He asked her out on several occasions and she condescendingly replied that she would not date a "greaser" (this was the title given to that minority of students who openly admitted and displayed their contempt for school and society). The rejection only inspired him to more dramatic measures to win her love. She too had a job after school, and one evening he waited for her after work. To his delight she drove home unescorted. Abandoning his timidity and ignoring her previous rejections, he followed her home, walked to the door, knocked, and introduced himself to her parents.

The family had moved to Florida from Alabama. Bonnie's mother had been born and reared in the deep South. Her father was full-blooded Cherokee Indian. A large but gentle man, it was his lineage which lent Bonnie her intriguing charm and beauty. Amid the introductions, Bonnie walked in and blushed, knowing she had been caught in deception. She had fended off Walter's advances by professing to have a steady date. Her parents, despite Bonnie's insistence that it was unnecessary, left the two alone.

The victory was the traditional one. A beautiful, disinterested girl wooed into love by the persistence and daring of her suitor. Soon they were caught in the grip of obsession. Each moment was devoted to courtship. Walter's mother permitted the use of a '64 Pontiac Tempest, and the automobile became a chariot for the two young lovers.

7

CHAPTER SEVEN

The summer months passed quickly and August brought the return of school and Walter's father. When Walter Sr. arrived home, he expected his son to be waiting for him. He was not. When he called Walter, he learned that "things had changed" and that his son had already made plans for the evening. Walter put the receiver down without saying goodbye to his father or telling him when he would come to see him. Since Bonnie did not get off work until later that night, he decided that his father deserved a belated welcome after all. "Why not?" he questioned himself. "Nothing better to do."

Walter walked into the house. His father emerged from the bedroom and took a seat on the long couch opposite Walter. He waited for his father to speak. Walter Sr. broke the silence by asking his son to stay for dinner, but the invitation was rejected. Walter Sr. then demanded that his son stay for dinner. Walter freed himself from the couch, sarcastically telling his father, "Watch me leave." Walter Sr. sat motionless. He had struggled throughout his stay in prison to keep his sanity. On the verge of an emotional breakdown, he saw his past as wasted. He hoped that at least his son would continue to breathe life into his weary frame. Upon finding Walter rebellious and hateful, he realized he had ruined more than one life.

With effort Walter Sr. lifted himself from the couch and stood silently. Then he grew angry and finally he snapped. His head crackled with an uncontrollable rage; his blood pressure rocketed. Rushing toward his son, he struck him to the floor.

"My God, what have I done?" he wailed. He reached down but Walter moved away and cupped his hand over his swelling eye. He had rarely seen his father cry. Now he watched him sobbing and clutching the arm that had delivered the blow. The sight disgusted him. Before he could release a mounting load of vitriolic his mother ordered him from the house.

"Don't come back until you give your father his respect," she screamed.

By the time Walter picked up Bonnie, his eye had closed. He explained what had taken place and she begged him to allow her to meet with his father. Somehow she felt responsible for the fight, and somehow, she believed, she might assist in a reconciliation. Walter was silent. She persisted in asking him to take her to meet his father, but he persisted in rejecting the idea. Though he wished to make her happy, he finally cut short her pleas with an emphatic "No!" His relationship to his father had been damaged permanently. It was not his father's actions that had caused the destruction. The painful blow he had delivered to his son was defensive, not offensive. Six months behind bars and Walter had never visited him. His father had asked to meet Bonnie. Walter denied the request. His father had struggled to find love in his eyes but found instead disrespect. It was these actions, his actions that precipitated the regrettable scene. His father's physical response was merely the empty fury of a broken and forgotten middle-aged man. He had destroyed his father. Bonnie searched his eyes for a hint of remorse or compassion. She found none.

Bonnie gave up for that night, but the alienation continued to nag at her. How could their love for each other prosper, when the love between father and son was broken? After several weeks Walter acquiesced and took Bonnie to meet his father. A few days later Walter informed his father that he was going to marry Bonnie. Walter Sr. was scheduled to leave for Oklahoma on business. Before the trip he exacted a promise from his son that he would not marry until his return several months later.

Although Walter and Bonnie spent hours together every day, as with most young lovers, their brief absences from each other could only be tolerated through note writing. One such note was intercepted by Bonnie's mother. It revealed that her daughter had been sleeping with Walter but was now committed to celibacy until marriage. Walter and Bonnie had pledged that they would stop sleeping together until after the wedding. Bonnie's mother was unaware of a wedding, and she was horrified by the revelation that her daughter had forfeited the flower of her youth unblessed by marriage vows. She called Walter Sr. in Oklahoma and told him about the note. He assured her that he would return immediately and end the relationship by moving his family to Oklahoma. He made the mistake of calling Walter to tell him of the move. That night Walter and Bonnie vowed that they would elope.

A rumor at school had it that a small town in Georgia allowed marriages of minors without parental consent. Believing the incredulous information, the couple boarded a Greyhound bus for Folkston, Georgia, on the day that Walter Sr. returned from Oklahoma.

Immediately upon exiting at the bus stop in Folkston, they ran into difficulties. A kind-looking policeman saw that the youngsters were a bit disoriented and asked them the nature of their visit. Both answered at the same time but not in accord. Walter stated that they were on their honeymoon. Bonnie offered that they had eloped. Unmoved by pleas that nothing was amiss, the officer decided that the best way to find out the truth was to call Bonnie's parents. In less than an hour they were on a bus going back to Miami.

Undaunted, they left the Miami bus station to check into a ten-dollar-a-night dive on Biscayne Boulevard. Bonnie's parents had assumed they would drive home after their exploit. They underestimated the persistence of first love.

Money was scarce. After a few nights Walter had to borrow from friends to pay for the dingy room. Two weeks of peanut butter and jelly was enough. He called his father and promised he would come home provided he and Bonnie were allowed to marry. His father agreed to the terms. A meeting was set up for that evening at the Ranch House Restaurant on 7th Avenue.

All Walter Sr.'s persuasion was unleashed on his son. Walter refused to budge. The older man turned to plead with Bonnie. Walter interrupted, demanding that Bonnie not be interrogated or become the object of a lecture.

One question was asked nonetheless. "Bonnie, have you and Walter been sleeping together?"

Bonnie put her head down. Walter Sr.'s big hands lay open across the table. His voice was hushed and steady when he spoke to his nineteen-year-old son, "Never, when I was your age, never once before marriage did I do that. I may be guilty of many things, but I never committed that sin . . . and I am disgusted and grieved – I can't look at you." He stormed to the car.

Bonnie's eyes were red from tears. She looked at Walter apologetically. Walter's mother stared at him in disbelief. "You finally did it, Walter; you finally broke your father's heart. God help you."

She turned toward Bonnie and in an acrimonious tone asked if Bonnie could separate herself from Walter for one night and go home. Walter grabbed Bonnie's arm and jerked her out of the restaurant booth. Back in the motel Bonnie cried through the night. Walter searched for words of consolation; they did not exist. He pulled the musty drapes open and stared at Biscayne Boulevard until the sun returned the next morning.

8

CHAPTER EIGHT

Walter Thiel Shaw, Jr., and Bonnie Helton were married in a Nazarene church located on 95th Street and 7th Avenue. Walter's aunt, uncle, younger sister, and parents were in attendance. Bonnie's mother was disgraced and remained at home. Several cousins, however, witnessed Bonnie's Cherokee father offer her in marriage.

Immediately after the ceremony the couple left for Oklahoma. Walter's father had a commitment from investors there to fund his electronic research. Oklahoma proved to be a dry run. A few weeks later Walter Sr. informed his family that they were going to Findley, Ohio. His new backer, an obstetrician by the name of Dr. Razor, owned Buckeye Communications.

After arriving in Findley, Bonnie began suffering from dizziness and nausea. An examination by Dr. Razor revealed that she was pregnant. At seventeen she hardly considered childbearing an enviable accomplishment. But Walter assured her that her position was, above all others, exalted.

On November 18, 1967, Walter Shaw, Jr., became a father.

The baby girl was named Michele Marie. After a recuperation period the young family returned to Miami, and Bonnie presented her newborn as an offering of reconciliation to her dejected mother.

While in Miami, Walter contacted an old buddy. They decided to make an excursion to Miami Beach. In order to be fashionable, and drifting back into old habits, they impulsively shoplifted a pair of swimsuits from Burdines department store. The two had raided clothes before, and though Walter had the money to purchase the trunks, he convinced himself that his money could be better spent. Before they reached their car a security guard apprehended them. Embarrassed, Walter attempted to pay on the spot, but the officer insisted that such a settlement was impossible. Walter was arrested. His first incarceration lasted only a few hours. The entire fiasco seemed ironic. Married and content, he had transformed himself from thug to father and now, as a father, he was being arrested. His desire to brutalize society had been temporarily soothed with the balm of love, yet he was being punished for a prank. He and Bonnie drove back to Findley, Ohio, after Christmas to discover that Walter Sr. had created the world's first conference call. The device allowed conversation on one line for more than two people. The commercial potential of the conference call was huge. Walter Sr. decided to break with Buckeye Communications and join two entrepreneurs, Oscar Blevitt and Mel Adler, who told him that they had the capital to market the unit. The new company was incorporated under the name Com-u-trol. Operations were transferred to Miami. The contract between Walter Shaw, Sr., and his two partners included a fifty-fifty stock split with one-third of the voting rights going to the inventor and a fifty-fifty royalty-sharing agreement for life. Adler and Blevitt also gained rights in two of Walter Sr.'s upcoming inventions – divert-a-call and extend-a-wats. In addition to royalties and stock, Walter Sr. was paid a handsome salary.

With the understanding that his son would enroll in college, Walter Sr. bought him a brand-new '68 Camaro. Walter passed his GED test and started classes at Dade Junior College. With his new automobile and with a beautiful wife and daughter at home, he began to ponder the possibility of fulfilling his father's dream for him to become a doctor or lawyer. Out of necessity, his schoolwork competed with a forty-hour-a-week job at Schiff's Shoe Store. He worked on the floor as a salesman, earning minimum wage plus a small commission. His father added a hundred dollars each week to enrich his scant salary. Still concerned, and willing to go to any length to keep his son in school, Walter Sr. purchased a '59 Corvette for his daughter-in-law. Though she might have chosen a myriad of different ways to express her thanks, she could only offer him another grandchild. The untimely pregnancy did not amuse Walter's father, and he made the conditions of his benevolence clear: "Walter, I will not pay for every child you have!"

To meet the needs that the unborn would soon require, Bonnie took a job with an insurance agency and left Michele with her grandmother. Walter, impetuous as always, overloaded himself with sixteen hours of school, and that to be shared with his duties as a husband, father, and shoe salesman.

One night he came home to learn that Bonnie's employer at the insurance agency had attempted the ignoble act of seduction. Enraged, he terminated her contract on the spot. Exhausted and frustrated by holding down a job and going to school, he declared an end to his educational endeavors too. Having experienced both poverty and wealth, he resolved to never again live in poverty. He correctly appraised the academic road as rewarding but long. With an expectant wife and a growing daughter he could not wait another day, much less four years, to achieve success. His father had refused to support him unconditionally and his life-style had become pleasureless and burdensome. He wanted to accommodate himself with all of life's choicest treasures. There was only one way to acquire wealth quickly as far as he knew. Of course, this method, like any other overnight-success scheme, would be risky, but he had seen it done before.

That night he could not sleep. He was excited. Though he would not articulate it, he knew that he had already made a decision. On the threshold of a new direction, one for which there would be no return, he eyed the telephone. Without picking up the receiver he dialed a number just to see how it might feel. Several quiet minutes later he lifted the receiver and dialed slowly. It was a long-distance call. He heard the phone ring. Taking a deep breath, he committed. His last thought before speaking into the receiver was simple – *I have no other choice*. Then someone answered and Walter raised his voice. "Uncle Archie?"

9

CHAPTER NINE

A close friend of Walter's had recently stolen $5,000 in money orders. Unable to carry his crime through to completion, he looked to Walter for help. Walter accepted the opportunity as easy and profitable. He proceeded to cash the money orders and was immediately arrested. He hired criminal attorney Paul Pollack, and a one thousand dollar bond was made.

On the morning of the court hearing it seemed that Walter had gotten up on the right side of the bed. Ellen Marfonias, formerly an assistant to State Attorney Richard Gerstein, had been elevated to the bench. She had been recused from the iniquitous trial that resulted in his father's imprisonment. Perhaps she felt she owed the father one, but regardless of motivation, she withheld adjudication of guilt and placed Walter on a probation period of three years for a crime that commonly warranted three to five years' incarceration. His only obligation was to repay the $5,000. Before Walter left the courtroom Judge Marfonias promised him that the leniency she had shown would disappear if he ever stood before her again.

Ignoring her warning, that same week he entangled himself in another illegal operation. He had been introduced to Carl Miller, and over dinner Walter learned that he had something for which Miller would pay top dollar, the black box. He promised Miller as many as he needed at $1,500 a unit, plus $5,000 up front. Carl Miller agreed to the per-unit price but insisted that payment would not be received until delivery. Future earnings hardly relieved the pressure for the immediate repayment of the $5,000, and to be delinquent could result in a trip to prison. Miller, seeing Walter's desperation, offered him a job on the side to earn additional money. Miller's corporation, known as Standard Plastering Company, was merely a front for criminal activities. Miller was no petty criminal. He was an important cog in south Florida's Mafia machine. Walter's work involved a man even more powerful – Frank Sacco.

Sacco, a brutal extortionist, was headquartered in New York, but his "business" stretched to south Florida and beyond. Miller pushed Sacco to hire Walter as a courier. Sacco had Walter fly to New York to learn the nature of the job. He was to carry an attache´ case three times a week from Miami International Airport to La Guardia in New York via JFK on Long Island. Once at La Guardia, Shaw was to purchase a locker, place the attache´ case in it, and then walk into the men's restroom. Inside the restroom, one of Sacco's henchmen would hand him $500 in exchange for the key.

Though knocking down $1,500 a week, Walter was too late to repay his father. Walter Sr. lost his stock in Com-u-trol. When he needed cash to protect himself from the takeover, there was none to be found. He forfeited his holdings shortly before Walter began his financial rise.

A lust for money was now competing for the intense amorous attention he had been giving to Bonnie and the hatred that had been submerged during the first few months of marriage surfaced. He moved his family into luxury accommodations at the Gulf Air apartment complex and showered Bonnie with gifts. His father, desperate after losing his stock, made the distasteful decision to provide his son with black boxes. While his father tottered on the verge of economic collapse, Walter spent with reckless abandon. His appetite for money was insatiable, and soon the $1,500 weekly take could not satisfy him. He wanted more.

One afternoon Walter sat in the comforts of a first-class seat, en route to La Guardia airport. Nervously glancing at the attache' case, he was assailed by two rival thoughts. Hectic and noisy, one impulse darted and flirted with his brain, urging him to open the attache' case. The other drove home like the somber downbeat of a funeral dirge, warning: *Don't look inside.*

Sacco had handed him one absolute rule. He was never to look inside the attache' case regardless of the circumstances. For three months he had found the command easy to follow. Now he was tormented, driven to unlock the case. The temptation became his master. He flicked the lever that released the two latches, and slowly pushed the case open. His eyes were flooded by a cool sea of green, more money than he had ever imagined. He made his way to the lavatory and carefully locked the door. Stooping down, he laid the attache' case across the toilet seat, opened it again, and began to count the money. His hands shook. He broke into erratic fits of laughter. At last he shut the case and closed his eyes. A quick count showed approximately $96,000. The enormous sum demanded action. Walter calmly returned to his seat with a plan.

When the jet landed at JFK, he deposited the attache´ case in a locker, walked outside, and caught a cab to La Guardia. While in the cab, he prepared himself for the critical phase of the heist. He would have to convince the pick-up man that he had been robbed. He knew his performance must achieve Academy Award caliber. If not, the failure would be costly. He concentrated on the situation, the familiar restroom, the thin, darkly dressed man.

By the time he reached La Guardia, he was perspiring. His back, forehead, neck, wrists, hands, ankles, feet, chest – every part of his body – began to protest his decision. He was nervous, excited. That was the beauty of the plan. Had he really been robbed he would have appeared equally disheveled. As he reached for the metal handle of the restroom door, a disconcerting thought blazed. He looked more than nervous, he looked worried and guilty. He was smoldering and it was too late to put out the fire. He approached the thin man in the restroom to explain what had happened. The man listened. His face showed no alarm. He instructed Walter to return to Miami until Sacco got word to him. He looked at Walter's shaking hands, gave him his payment, and walked out.

Walter peered at the spot where the nameless pick-up man had been standing. He tried to understand. How could it have been so easy? The man calmly accepted his answer, paid him, and lumbered out indifferently. No cross-examination, threats, or warnings, just business as usual. Walter examined his face in the mirror. He looked awful, pale and sickly. He surveyed the restroom. What had happened? He tried to comprehend the impact of the last hour – one tiny hour. He cupped his hands underneath the faucet, gulped down his fill and splashed the cold water across his face.

When he arrived in Miami, his father relayed the message that Carl Miller wanted to see him. Walter walked into Miller's warehouse afraid that his clever ploy had misfired. To his relief, Miller simply asked him to repeat the events related to the robbery.

His next meetings were with several car salesmen. He

bought Bonnie a white 454 Corvette with black leather interior and purchased a gold Coupe DeVille for himself, paying cash for both. A few nights later he and Bonnie, along with his mother, father, the ex-mayor of Hollandale, and his wife, met for dinner. He lavished his guests with food and spirits. After the meal, Walter's father left the table for some fresh air. The three women excused themselves and walked to the powder room. The ex-mayor and Walter sat across the table from each other laughing at the last joke. John Steele, the ex-mayor, Carl Miller's close friend, was exhausting his laugh. A deeply serious expression came to his face. The abrupt change startled Walter. Steele placed his hands around his plate and gazed at the leftover food. Without looking at Walter he warned him that the New York incident was not over. Walter responded that he did not know what he meant. Steele's eyes darted up to meet Walter's. He warned him again, "Walter, don't play games. What is all this? New cars, dinners, new clothes, come on, I know, and what's worse, Carl knows . . . Walter, they know – they've known. I just hope you're able to return the money."

Before Walter could speak, his father returned to the table, followed by his mother, Bonnie, and John Steele's wife. The dinner party continued its lively conversation while Walter's head began to throb. His gaze drifted toward Steele, who still carried the gravity of the matter in his eyes. By the end of the night, Walter's headache was tormenting.

The next morning he forced himself out of bed and into the bathroom. The drinks alone could not account for the pain. Feeling the urge, he spit into the sink and watched a crimson saliva linger around the drain. His stomach had assaulted itself. He dressed quietly and kissed Bonnie as she lay in bed. As he cranked the Coupe DeVille, he remembered the blood he had spit up. He needed to check with a doctor. Instead he drove to a gun shop. After consulting with the salesman he decided on a .38 special. He slapped the Smith & Wesson into the palm of his hand a few quick times. "Careful," the employee laughed. "Too late," Walter replied smiling. "Too late for that."

10

CHAPTER TEN

Walter carried his .38 special at all times, but after several weeks the fear that had harassed him as a result of John Steele's warnings began to play a lesser role in his life. He no longer watched people suspiciously, nor did he check his car before getting into it at night. As the fear subsided, the urge to spend money surged again.

His visits to the horse tracks demanded more resources as his confidence in luck increased and his better judgment declined. His tailored clothes and patent leather shoes became mere accessories. Exhilaration came from treating his companions to dinner, drinks, and good times. He placated Bonnie by providing her with material possessions she had previously resigned herself to only dream about.

One afternoon, when Walter arrived at the track eager to join his friends, he ran into Harry Freedman and Roger Missio, in addition to the usual crowd. The two well-dressed men were henchmen for Frank Sacco. Walter recognized them immediately. They greeted him pleasantly, and in the course of conversation Walter asked them why they had come to Miami.

They replied that Frank had allowed them a few weeks' vacation, and with the weather cold up north, they decided to spend some time with Carl Miller in the warmth of the Florida sun. They casually remarked that Walter seemed to be doing well for himself. He searched their faces to see if they bore any malice against him. He found only smiles.

A few days later the phone rang as Walter was shaving. He had slept till noon. Still groggy, he picked up the receiver to hear Miller's voice. Miller was jovial and invited him out to the warehouse for a meeting and a late lunch. Walter put the .38 special in the glove compartment of the Corvette, on the passenger's side, and ripped through the gears as he sped to Miller's warehouse on the north side of Miami.

He eased onto the dirt driveway that led to the warehouse and parked just inside a chain-link fence. Miller was standing on the loading dock. Harry Freedman and Roger Missio, whom he had last seen at the track, walked out to meet him. He said hello, joined them, and after a few steps realized that the men on either side of him had not come to welcome him. He turned back toward his car, remembering his gun, and felt a firm hand clamp on his arm. Before he could free himself from Roger's hold, Harry Freedman grabbed his other arm, "No, not today, kid – if it ain't on you, you're out of luck."

Miller sat in an executive's chair, resting way back, with his feet propped up on his desk. He clicked his tongue against the roof of his mouth and shook his head as Walter was led into the room.

"Walter, that is a b-e-a-u-tiful white Corvette. I understand you also have a gold Coupe DeVille. In fact, the boys tell me you've been frequenting the tracks lately. And let me compliment you on your choice of clothing. Peter Kent? Walter, you look sharp, very sharp. I've just got one question. Where did you get the money? You're not delivering as much as you used too. You know, if I didn't know better, I would think that you had inherited $96,000!"

Feigning anger, Walter asked him what his last remark meant. Miller answered by snapping his fingers. Upon this cue Walter was dragged from the room and out of the warehouse.

After hitting the ground he felt the blunt point of a wing-tip shoe drive into his ribs and then another into his mouth. He opened his lips to release a mouthful of blood as the same shoe hammered systematically at each rib. His nose bent flat as another stinging kick was delivered. This last blow turned him over on his back. Roger straddled him and began to slam his fist into his face. Walter faded long before the punishment ended. Miller called the assailants off and thanked them for their courteous visit.

Walter opened his eyes, his body motionless. His mauled face had collected grains of sticky, bloodstained sand. Feeling only the deadness in his head, he rolled over on his stomach and pulled his hands underneath his chest to push himself from the ground. His knees slid up to provide support, and he started crawling toward the white Corvette. His watch said 3:00 P.M. He had been out for over an hour. The glare of the intense Miami sun blinded him. His body had been mutilated and the sharp jagged pain in his sides made crawling torturous. Periodically, he opened his swollen lips to allow blood to flow. After fumbling clumsily inside his car for several seconds, the gun fell from the glove compartment. Picking it up, he used the car as leverage to force his body into an upright position. The bright sunlight added to his disorientation. He thought he heard a loud metallic whining all around him. It was as if the very earth began to call, as if mosquitoes had covered every inch of land and screaming an angry shriek in unison. He stumbled, caught his balance, and staggered back toward the warehouse. The tormenting whine grew more fierce. When he approached the building, he heard a woman's voice. The eerie sound ceased.

Sitting at a secretary's desk was Michie, Miller's wife. She looked at him, shocked. His shirt was matted with a mixture of blood and dirt. Waving the .38 high over his head, he demanded that she produce her husband. She began to cry and told Walter that he had left for the day. The story did not pass. Walter pointed her toward Miller's office door with a motion of his gun. Miller sat up straight. Walter, swaying in the doorway, pointed the pistol barrel directly toward Miller's gut. Even a wounded man would not miss at such a short distance. Sucking for more breath, Walter screamed, "I'm going to kill you."

Michie cried out. Miller commanded her to shut up, then looked at Walter, smiling. "Walter, you're not going to kill nobody. You know you did wrong. I know you did wrong and Frank knows you did wrong. You're not going to kill someone that you just robbed, and I'll tell you something you already know. If you kill me, there will be five more where I come from. This is a simple situation. You broke the rules, and out of respect to your dad we let you live, *and because you enjoy living,* you'll return the $96,000."

"You'll burn in hell before I pay that money. I'm going to kill you, man." Walter came back angrily.

"No, son. You pay or your daddy won't be able to save you," Miller said. He snapped his fingers and asked Michie to go get a steak. "Walter, we're gonna get a big steak for your eye. I'm gonna prepare you a shot of whiskey, and best of all, you're gonna sit down here, relax, and forget about this mess, it's over."

Miller removed the gun from Walter's fingers, eased him into a chair, and handed him a shotglass full of whiskey. "Drink up, we're gonna cool you off and then you're gonna return our money because you broke the rules. One thing, Walt, either the

$96,000 or your life." Carl turned, walked behind hid desk, and sat down. He propped his feet up and smile at Walter. "You'll feel better once you get this thing off your shoulders, kid."

11

CHAPTER ELEVEN

At 7:45 that night Walter regained enough strength to leave. He remembered that he and Bonnie had promised to eat dinner with his parents so he drove to their house. Everyone was busy in the kitchen when he arrived. He opened the front door, and quickly headed for his old bedroom and stretched out across the small bed. Bonnie called out as soon as she heard him. No answer – she went to check on him.

"Don't turn on the lights, I have a splitting headache," he moaned.

"Honey, what's wrong? Your mother and I have cooked dinner for you and . . ."

He interrupted, "I don't feel well."

Bonnie flipped the light switch, "Oh my God, Walter!" she cried out.

Walter Sr. and Betty Lou rushed in. Walter Sr. stormed around the room, demanding to know who had beaten his son beyond recognition. Walter sat up slowly. There was no use in trying to hide the truth. It would be on the street by midnight. He confessed the $96,000 theft and the subsequent lashing.

Walter Sr. was enraged, his son had violated the rules all right, but Miller was a greater violator and the latter, a seasoned veteran, knew better. Walter Sr. pointed toward the telephone, called out Miller's home number, and ordered Bonnie to dial. When Miller answered, she began screaming out warnings to him about the consequences of his actions. She yelled until the phone was pried from her ear. Walter Sr. did not waste words or issue warnings. He demanded a meeting.

Shortly after 9:00 P.M., Walter and his father arrived at Lum's Restaurant in Opalocka. Walter Sr. was infuriated, boiling. His eyes watered. His heavy voice shook as he spoke. He looked as though he were ready to spill over or catch fire at any moment. He informed Miller that upon suspecting his son he had had a choice. He could have called a "sit-down" to determine whether or not Walter was guilty, or he could have beaten him. Since he chose to punish him before he had been proven guilty, he had forfeited the $96,000. (A sit-down is an official procedure taken by the Mafia to settle disputes among members. In a sit-down the accused and his accuser come before a committee of men who rule on the case. Miller's decision to beat Walter was a serious breach of Mafia etiquette.)

"You beat Walter, so Sacco is paid – period!" Walter Sr. blasted. The two men faced off. Miller had been ordered by Sacco to use Walter as an example to others who attempted similar stunts.

"You don't just walk off with $96,000. We're not running a bank; your kid's gotta learn his respect – that's the way it works," Miller protested.

"Walter's been beat, Sacco's paid," Walter Sr. responded, slamming his hand down on the table.

Miller stood up and looked at Walter Sr. in exasperation, waiting, as if to make a prophetic pronouncement, but unable to speak, he turned and left.

Later that night Walter checked into a hospital emergency room. The doctors were appalled. A mere nineteen-year-old boy had been beaten nearly to death. They would have been stupefied had they known that this same nineteen-year-old had lifted almost $100,000 from one of the country's most ruthless extortionists. The examination showed that Walter's ribs had been broken, and his head carried a severe concussion and possibly scars. Bonnie, swollen with child, went to comfort her young husband.

12

CHAPTER TWELVE

The extortion money Walter delivered to New York each week carried a heavy price tag. Money on the streets was available at twelve-percent interest a week. After two weeks a $1,000 loan becomes a $1,254 debt. To protect themselves against delinquent debtors, loansharks enact severe penalties. Those debtors who fail to meet their deadlines face broken bones, dismemberment, or death. The FBI had been monitoring several people who had allegedly gone to the streets for capital. One unfortunate Miami Beach nightclub owner under surveillance failed to meet his payment. He was gunned down. The FBI had watched the man for several months and with mounting evidence, plus a homicide, they felt confident enough to make arrests and go to trial. They indicted Frank Sacco, Carl Miller, and Harry Freedman. A federal marshal was sent to deliver a subpoena to Walter. The mission was futile. He had disappeared.

Fearing the consequences of court, Walter hid in a dilapidated little house in Hollywood, Florida. To testify meant death. Tucked away, he promised Bonnie safety. A few days later he was discovered. Somehow Carl Miller had located him. Miller spoke to him briefly and complimented him on finding an adequate hideaway. Miller's message was expected: Stay out of sight until the trial is over – a course of action Walter had already initiated. Walter swore allegiance and asked him how he had located the place. Miller replied, "We always know, no matter where you are, we know. It may take a while, but we connect. Kid, we all made bond, Frank, Harry, and myself. But things are bad on us. That $96,000 deal is history. This is your job now, Walt. Don't show up if you want to stay healthy." Walter acquiesced for a second time and wished him luck.

The trial proceedings turned into a bloodbath. In Tampa a government witness was being led up the federal court building steps. Before he reached the top of the steps, he was down – shot down by a nineteen-year-old sniper using a high-powered rifle, from the roof of a nearby building. No one was safe. Several other witnesses met a similiar grisly fate. When the young rooftop executioner agreed to confess that he had been hired by Frank Sacco, his jail cell became his casket. The shortened sentence he had hoped to receive in exchange for information was granted in record time. His prison stay turned out to be but a few nights. It was not prison officials who released him, however. One morning he was let out of jail the hard way. He had been murdered – he was out of time and life. His decision to deal with the Feds was no bargain.

The blood extracted from these incidents led a gruesome trail to a notorious organization founded by Frank Sacco, Albert Anastasia, Tom Palmer, and Bugsy Segal. The operation was given the accurate title "Murder, Inc." Their revolting entrepreneurship specialized in contract murders, and when Sacco was indicted, the FBI learned that he had an efficient and brutal method of legal defense. He did not allow witnesses to make it to the stand.

One afternoon a black Lincoln Town Car approached Walter's lean-to-style home. From it emerged Frank Sacco. He informed Walter that the trial would last longer than expected. His camouflaged existence would have to be maintained. The delay was due to the fact that Carl Miller had turned state's witness, a problem Sacco was "working on." Walter had good reason to believe Sacco did not trust him to stay quiet either.

A few weeks earlier he and his father had been instructed to meet at 163rd Street in North Miami. Walter made the trip and met Vinnie De' Angelo. De' Angelo had gained a national reputation as one of organized crime's smoothest terminators. He wore mirror sunglasses and $1,000 suits. His eyes were cold and frightening. Though he had seen much carnage in his life, he had never been in a war. The bloodshed he had witnessed had been caused by his own hands. He derived pleasure from his craft but did not, however, allow the sadistic ecstasy he received from taking human life interfere with his professionalism. He was not a psycho. He was efficient and immensely satisfied by being the best. His talk with Walter was not dramatic. It was businesslike. "You have one week to produce the $96,000. If not, you will end up in Biscayne Bay."

The confrontation made the recent visit by Sacco seem odd. De' Angelo never returned, as evidenced by the fact that Walter was in Hollywood, Florida, and not at the bottom of Biscayne Bay. How strange that Sacco, who had obviously sent De' Angelo to press him, would show up. Something was awry.

Though the days were monotonous, Walter's tiny hidaway was in the eye of a hurricane. All around him the world was churning. Sacco ordered more deaths, and witnesses involuntarily followed his dreadful orders. The FBI struggled to keep its case alive.

The threat upon Walter's life by one of the mob's heavy hitters was weeks overdue. Curiosity twitched in Walter's brain, but he knew there were only two important considerations to remember. One, he was lucky to be alive. De' Angelo did not make idle threats. Usually, in fact, he made no threats at all. Two, survival demanded that he remain in the eye of the storm. To venture out would mean getting sucked in beyond his control. Such spinning flight would lead to a collision with someone powerful, someone who would kill him.

13

CHAPTER THIRTEEN

Since the Sacco trial was to be delayed, Walter combed the classified ads for cash-generating opportunities. He found a podiatrist, Dr. Arnold Landsman, who was looking for a financial partner. Landsman owned Black Bird Stud Farm near Ocala and needed someone who could buy into thirty-three brood mares, at $2,500 each. Walter figured the investment could be profitable if handled properly. His first move was to contact Bob Hornstein. Hornstein specialized in fraudulent land schemes according to Walter. His most successful venture involved selling gold bonds to senior citizens on property in Volusia County that was underwater. Walter made a deal with Hornstein to use some of the worthless real estate certificates as collateral for his negotiations with Landsman. His preliminary meetings with Dr. Landsman were circuslike displays of wealth. Walter transformed himself from nineteen going on twenty to thirty going on thirty-five. Landsman was impressed, and Walter's offer to buy in with real estate as collateral was accepted. He had overwhelmed the older man with his stylish suits, beautiful car, and generous spirit.

The relationship between Walter and Dr. Landsman remained amicable throughout the next year. When Walter learned that the trial had ended and Frank Sacco was sentenced to fifty-five years while Carl Miller was given just twelve months at Eglin Air Force Base, he dissolved the partnership, came out of hiding, and carted his family back to Miami. *(Later that year Frank Sacco had his "attorney" visit him in jail wearing a fake beard and a wig. Sacco exchanged clothes with his "attorney," put on the wig and beard, and walked out of the Hillsborough County jail. He enjoyed his cleverly earned freedom for one year before being arrested in New York. A federal court judge there determined that Sacco was beyond rehabilitation and gave him twenty consecutive years on top of the previous sentences. The brutal extortionist did not escape again.)*

With Walter's determination to develop a new money-making strategy, a revelation had emerged from the Landsman partnership. The contrast between lifting $96,000 from the Mafia and taking from a legitimate business-man was striking. Walter had cleaned Landsman to the bone, and the good doctor did not break his ribs, nor did he split his skull. Dr. Landsman, all said and done, was quite helpless. The legitimate business world, that was where the easy money was, especially for such a firm believer in social Darwinism. Although Walter had never heard of that combination of words, he certainly knew their meaning. Survival of the fittest was a worthy creed for him. The twenty-year-old decided his talent was entrepreneurship and, equipped with the two essential qualities for making a fast buck, charm and ruthlessness, he was ready.

An old friend, Dick Ronco, contacted Walter. They met at a flea market. Ronco had no financial advice. He did, however, offer a story which proved interesting. It seemed another friend of Ronco's had come down from New York to make a hit on a

Florida "kid." Ronco described his friend as the most savage and expert hit man in the business. The trip turned into tragedy, at least for Ronco's friend. Before liquidating his victim, he had been shot and killed by a south Florida cowboy in a bar. Vinnie De' Angelo, the merciless, had been wasted by a country cowboy. Suddenly Walter knew why Sacco had personally visited him. The hit on Walter was off because the hitter was dead. Walter told Ronco about his involvement with De' Angelo. Ronco shook his head. "You're lucky, Walt, real lucky."

"No, don't you get it?" Walter replied with a teasing smile. "I'm unstoppable."

14

CHAPTER FOURTEEN

(The personality introduced at this point cannot be identified by name. In 1987 the national media brands him as one of the two most powerful men in organized crime. It is suggested that he could be the first boss of the bosses since Carlo Gambino. For this biography, the author has given him the pseudonym "The Bear.")

After his return to Miami Walter's father explained that he had hired someone to recover the valuable stock that had been swindled from him by Adler and Blevitt. Walter Sr. went on to tell his son that The Bear was a powerful mafioso in south Florida. Walter scoffed. "Dad, they all say they're it – 'I'm the big man, I'm connected with so-and-so' they say. These guys are frauds, losers."

A few days later he met The Bear. The Bear was heavily built, not obese, but muscular. His body was a one-sized, uniform, bulky square from head to toe. Despite his massive frame, his head seemed larger still. It was a block head, a bullish head. His somewhat oily hair was parted to the side. He stared indifferently, devoid of emotions. Ironically, in spite of disproportionate physical components, he was handsome. Although only in his late thirties, there was, perhaps flowing from his dark eyes, an energy, an authority, usually reserved for an older man, an ancient warrior. Walter conceitedly ignored the awesome presence, mistaking the occasion as an opportunity to flex his ego by taming The Bear. "You're the big guy, huh? Is that what you say? You're the Man?" he chided.

Walter Sr. tried to interrupt, but Walter persisted. "Who are you with, you know – connected to?"

The Bear stirred and slammed his knuckles on the desk with a crack. Walter watched the veins jump from The Bear's wrist across his hand to his fingers. Gazing at Walter menacingly, he spoke. His voice was soft, but deeply resonant. "Come here, son . . . closer." Walter obeyed. "Now see, I don't know what you mean by connected. My hand, sure, my hand is connected to my wrist and my wrist is connected to my arm and my arm is connected to my shoulder. I'm connected like that, but what you're talking about, no, I don't know."

Walter said nothing. For the first time in his life he had confronted raw power, a man whose authority lay not in his verbiage but in his eyes. *This was the Big Man.* Walter had to know him better. He needed to learn about power. How did you get it? How did you show it?

The Bear was slowly climbing the precarious ladder to the top of organized crime's hierarchical structure, along with a list of "young" Mafia hopefuls. The competition was ruthless. Once on the ladder, one did not resign and climb down. One survived or died. Walter had already tasted firsthand the savagery of Frank Sacco. Walter also knew about Tom Palmer, a bloodthirsty despot who would later befriend him. But Sacco and Palmer paled before The Bear. It was strange though, few people had heard of him. He was not flashy, always on the move, quietly moving, and never boisterous. By the time a person knew his name, it was too late. His bloodlettings were the only publicized part of his life. The street had it that he had blown one man apart with a handgun in a crowded elevator.

There had been many others, the street said, but The Bear did not talk. Some said that he had even played a role in Jimmy Hoffa's disappearance. How large a role was unknown but there was one distinct Bear trademark – Hoffa was gone. The Bear was allergic to evidence. He made sure none was around.

Walter studied The Bear, learning his moves, listening to what he said, and more important, feeding on his presence. A close friendship developed. The stocky mobster enjoyed Walter's bombast and began to take a fatherly interest in him. Occasionally he tried to steer him on a different course: "You don't have what it takes, you have a family that loves you – you know love. Quit trying to be so tough."

The Bear's advice was spurned. Walter refused to turn back. He wanted to be submerged in crime, be an intricate part of it, and perhaps, if he carefully imitated The Bear, he could become a leader. He wanted power, finger-snapping, people-jumping, and head-cracking power. He had found a new mentor to replace Uncle Archie. The Bear was better. He was deadly. Walter was ready to begin.

15

CHAPTER FIFTEEN

In recounting a life as multifaceted as Walter Shaw's, it is easy to fall prey to anachronisms. Events occurred simultaneously and the narrative becomes hectic, given the importance of each drama.

Walter had been studying the subtle nuances of power and intimidation under the tutelage of The Bear for a full year before opportunity passed his way and he was introduced to an expert of a very different kind. This expert was the best at his craft and had been trained by yet another master. After having practiced his inherited craft for a few years, the expert sought an heir to wear the crown of Master Jewel Thief. Twenty-year-old Walter Shaw was anointed.

Peter Joseph Salerno was the most adept jewel thief in the nation. He learned his trade, he told Walter, from Frank Davis. Davis had been trained at the courtesy of the United States Government during World War II by the secret service. The service recruited a select group of men to carry out very dangerous and important missions. Hitler's war machine was decimating Europe, and the United States recognized that defeating so capable a foe required more than military might. It required information detailing Hitler's war plans. The secret service began training men to infiltrate heavily guarded Nazi headquarters to gather information. Men were chosen who exhibited a natural aptitude for burglary. Davis passed muster and began his training. The procedures were thorough and arduous. The men were clued into every detail, regardless of how minuscule, that might thwart their forced entry into Nazi headquarters. They were shown how to approach lighted and unlighted windows without being spotted. Shoes, socks, pants, shirts, and tools were all specially selected. They could scamper across dimly lit yards without throwing a shadow or making a sound. Finger and foot-prints were intolerable. After many long sessions and months of instructions, the men went to perform their skills in Germany. The buildings they burglarized were as new to them as the countryside. The only familiarity they had with their surroundings came from photographs they had studied. Still, the excellence of their crafty execution conquered all obstacles.

After the war, Davis, like many war veterans, returned to ticker-tape parades and unemployment. Civilian life was boring and hunger was a nagging companion. Davis took the skills he had been taught and utilized them to fill his belly. Before long, his weekly take could have fed thousands, and after a few years he had become a millionaire, retiring to an elegant home in upper New York State.

Meanwhile, one of New York City's young thugs had earned a glowing reputation among the criminal element for assaulting and nearly killing a policeman in broad daylight as a favor to a friend. To repay young Salerno for his bold attack, the friend introduced him to Davis. Davis approved of Salerno and took him under his wing for one year, tutoring him in the fine art of burglary. Davis poured into Salerno his government training and experience and its practical application in civilian life. Davis warned him that the light thrown from a window causes a shadow to fall even when one stands beyond it. Windows must be approached slowly and at certain angles. Details, a million details, were gleaned from the old master, and though Salerno took part in operations that netted as much as $700,000 in one night, he was paid $300 a week. This was the apprentice stipend, and as any good apprentice knows, the value is not in the pay but in the education. Salerno learned patiently. The education would soon be worth millions.

Within a few years Salerno too had become a millionaire. His work continued unhindered. At thirty-seven, he moved to Florida to retire in a warm and hospitable climate. It had been eighteen years since he had first met Davis, almost two decades of excitement and opulence. Both Davis and Salerno had received their training free of charge from the government, and both men enjoyed vast fortunes, tax-free. Uncle Sam was generous.

Walter had been introduced to the elusive Pete Salerno by Carl Miller during his sojourn as an extortion-money courier. When Walter returned to Miami from Ocala, the two met again. Salerno recalled Miller's description of Walter: "The kid's crazy. He's got no fear, no sense of up and down, he's nineteen and he thinks he's the godfather."

Salerno wistfully remembered another pugnacious and egotistical kid from the streets of New York. He made a good jewel thief. The fond recollection of his youth brought a smile. Shaw would make a good thief too, he mused.

The proposition had been put before him. Walter needed work. Salerno gave the green light, and Shaw's training began. His first hands-on experience came in December of 1969. The target was a million-dollar home on the Intercoastal Waterway north of Miami.

It was a cold December night, but Walter was warmed by a flush of pride. His father, he was sure, was the best telephone inventor since Bell. He had to carry on the tradition. His childhood hero, Archie Geanunzio, had been the nation's largest bookie. Walter himself had worked for one of the nation's largest loansharks, and though his beating was brutal, he had taken satisfaction in knowing he had heisted $96,000 from such a dangerous figure. He had guts. Hadn't he shrugged off a threat by the most notorious hit man in crime? De' Angelo went down. They would all fall. Fate had chosen Walter. He was being coddled by The Bear, a vicious and rising powerbroker. Walter suspected that he did not know the half of The Bear's influence. Now, in addition to this friendship with the south Florida mobster, he sat at the feet of Pete Salerno, the undisputed kingpin of jewel thieves.

16

CHAPTER SIXTEEN

The first and most important principle in a successful heist was the "Dinnertime Principle." Salerno only visited the "rich and famous" while they were eating their caviar and sipping their champagne on weekend evenings. The decision to visit at that hour was shrewd. The wealthy elite from whom he stole kept their most valuable jewelry in bank safety-deposit boxes during the week. On weekends lovely ladies brought their prizes home to display on their evenly tanned bodies. The gala weekend festivities demanded all the pomp, circumstance, and pride they could invoke. The "Weekend Dinnertime Principle" produced the best results; however, it was by no means a steadfast rule. Weeknights too generated profits, and a smart thief worked these nights as well. But the ideal time was the weekend.

Dinnertime was a good time to work. The victims somehow felt secure while eating. After all, it would have been a gross vulgarity for someone to interrupt an evening meal. Lights were usually on throughout the house, making it impossible for those on the inside to see anything except their reflection when looking out a window, while Salerno and company, undetected, had a full panoramic view.

The family was centrally located as well, specifically around the dinner table. Moreover, dinner produced noise, and though the prim and proper would never admit it, they made "eating sounds." The chomping, chewing, and gulping reduced audio capabilities. Combined with eating sounds were laughter, talking, or on occasion arguments. Noise was noise, and the furor that accompanied the evening meals was a valuable asset in Salerno's trade.

Dusk also found doors unlocked. The family was busy eating, waiting to begin the evening, and consequently there was no need to lock doors.

Surprise may have been the most effective tool in Dinnertime burglaries. There was none. Everyone was already home. No one would be mysteriously pulling into the driveway, and the less variables the better, just as with anything scientific. Scientific indeed. No doubt about it, Salerno was a master at his craft. Shaw had joined a cadre of men, led by Salerno, better at burglary than any before or after them. The media had appropriately branded them the "Dinnertime Burglars." It was comical. Salerno had never once in his eighteen years of work been so much as arrested, and although the name "Dinnertime Burglars" may suggest frivolity, the victims were left humorless and jewelless.

The raiding party usually consisted of four people, a driver, two lookout men, and the actual break-in man. On occasion, five men would be employed and two would enter the house. One lookout man was always positioned in the front of the house. Should an unexpected visitor arrive the lookout could immediately alert his companions in back. The lookout man behind the house monitored its inhabitants. If anything went wrong, it was his job to alert the break-in man

The right attire was essential. Each man wore two layers of clothes. Underneath black slacks and a dark turtleneck were dress slacks and a dress shirt. If a burglar was identified, or an alarm went off and the driver was late for the pick-up, to be caught wearing black slacks and a dark turtleneck sweater would be fatal. Shoes played an important role. The best shoes were Clark Wallabees. The combination earth shoes– desert boots had two distinct advantages. First, they provided excellent traction. More important, they made it hard for police investigators to get prints. They left ambiguous, useless tracks.

A Dinnertime Man never carried ID. Murphy's Law, which states that if something can go wrong, it will go wrong, is especially applicable in a burglary. A dash out of the house and through the woods could very well empty pockets. To lose an ID. at the scene of a crime would probably mean prison.

Often the men would finish a job and find themselves stranded on the side of the road. The driver may have been delayed, and to prevent a vagrancy arrest each man carried several hundred dollars in cash. If a highway patrol officer pulled up, the burglar explained that he had lost his wallet a few days earlier. "Any cash on you?" would be the patrolman's question. If the burglar had none, he was booked for vagrancy.

The tools of the trade were simple. A Craftsman pry bar, a Buck penknife, a penlight and a packet of chewing gum made up the entire arsenal. The pry bar and penknife were effective means of entry. The penlight, though small, greatly enhanced vision. Its batteries were inserted with glove-covered hands. Such a small item was easily dropped, and if the forensics department found the shell of the penlight printless, they checked the batteries. This detail was commonly overlooked by burglars, but Dinnertime Men benefited from highly specialized government training. No detail was left to chance. The chewing gum relieved the men of ever-present cotton-mouth.

The pressure of the job wrung the mouth free of all saliva. After a while the situation became unbearable. Chewing gum was a needed salve.

Two critical pieces of equipment went on first and last, respectively. Brown or black cotton garden gloves went on before anything else, and the ski mask, which covered all but the eyes, was put on a few minutes before leaving the car. The same gloves and mask were never worn twice.

John Donaldson was the driver. Walter and Pete's brother-in-law, Dominic Latella, were the lookouts, and Pete was the break-in man.

On the night of Walter's first outing, Donaldson dropped the three men off five blocks from a lavish Fort Lauderdale home. It was 6:30 P.M. The sun had disappeared. Donaldson was to return in forty-five minutes. If the men were not there, he was to return every fifteen minutes until they showed. The three men approached the house. Pete's behavior, Walter observed, was not at all what he had imagined. In spite of Pete's verbal instructions to the contrary, Walter somehow still expected SWAT team – style maneuvering. Pete chewed his gum calmly. Latella stood behind a corner tree watching the road and the front of the house. Walter warily traced Pete's steps to the back.

The gentle waves of the Intercoastal Waterway did not lull or calm his nerves. His mind seemed one second away from short circuit. After a quick dog-check proved negative, Pete grabbed Walter's wrist firmly and steered him window to window. He approached each window five feet away from its square light projection and off to the side. At this angle windows had to be examined twice, once from each side, to get a complete view. Next, Walter was told to stand about twenty yards from the house. Only then did the beauty of Salerno's art come through.

It was Friday night. A four member family sat to leisurely relish their sumptuous evening meal. Walter could see each fork in its unaltered up-down-shoveling motion. He was seeing a bi-level movie. It was a farce. The family sat amid good food and conversation. When they laughed, Walter had to smile. If only they knew. Would they laugh so heartily? Would they find their conversation funny? Surely anyone could see the humor in this. Directly above their heads, as they cleaned their plates, Salerno was cleaning them out. It was like the plot from a Laurel-and-Hardy turned criminal series.

Suddenly Salerno emerged from the back door. There was a beef. Salerno's voice was urgent. The master bedroom was upstairs, and without a window it would only be accessible if he walked down a long corridor. Corridors were potential traps. The job would require finesse. "Every three minutes I'm coming out to check with you. If anybody leaves your line of vision, come in and get me," he whispered, his hands cupped around his mouth to direct the sound.

Come in? Walter's mask suddenly felt abrasive against his sweaty skin. Before he could respond, Salerno had darted back into the house. He tried to imagine the inside of the house. He could not. *Inside a strange house, unknown, every stick of furniture becomes a foil. Inside – enemy quarters, the owners know every inch of the house, the burglar knows nothing. Inside – down a long corridor, escape is impossible, the master bedroom becomes a giant lockbox. Inside – each breath carries such pitch.* "Can they hear me? They must hear me breathing." *Each footstep an alarm, sounds magnified and reverberating. Inside –* "Where are they? How long have I been here?"

Salerno dashed back out and Walter weakly signaled with his thumb and index finger. Back in again. Thirty minutes had elapsed since they had been dropped off. Walter paced unconsciously, then the dinner table began to clear. The family had finished. *"Go, no wait, go Walter go, no wait!"* He stood frozen. Then his dilemma disappeared. Out! Salerno was out with a white pillowcase stuffed full of goodies, just in time. Salerno had done it. He bounded toward Walter. This anti – Santa Claus was a victor again. They motioned for Latella and headed up the road. Walter's throat burned. He tried not to laugh. It was no use. He chuckled. "Fun, ain't it, kid?" whispered Pete as they hid roadside waiting for Donaldson.

"You look like Santa Claus," responded Walter.

Salerno shook his head, "This is the best Christmas you'll ever have, baby. This Santa don't bring Tinker Toys."

Donaldson pulled up and the three climbed in.

Later that night the men sat exploring the impressive pile of jewelry. "I took everything," Salerno said dryly. There were diamonds, gold, silver, pearls, and rubies.

"How much?" asked Walter between sips of beer. His hand shook around the cold can. Although elated, his nerves were still shot.

"About $85,000 easy," answered Pete. "Oh, I almost forgot. Here's your $300. Good work tonight, kid."

17

CHAPTER SEVENTEEN

After a few more scores in south Florida, Fort Lauderdale, Palm Beach, Boca Raton, Delray Beach, among others, the Dinnertime Burglars took their show on the road. Once they began the tour, Walter was included in a four-way split of the profits.

Their first performance was in the heart of Dixie. Deep in Alabama's rolling woods Salerno had pinpointed the estate of an heiress to one of the nation's largest industrial fortunes. For several decades the heiress had collected valuable jewels from every corner of the globe. The elegant southern colonial, though well-guarded, proved no match for the Dinnertime Carpetbaggers. It was ravaged of every jewel. These greedy invaders were loyal to neither North nor South. From Alabama they drove to Pennsylvania. Outside of Philadelphia is the Main Line, home to some of the oldest wealth in the country, dating back to the American Revolution. Salerno presented Walter with a grand tour of the scenic countryside, hitting twenty-seven estates in just two weeks. After the fence Walter's cut came to $500,000. He studied the mountainous pile of money, jaws agape, disbelieving.

After nearly getting killed over a paltry $96,000 at nineteen, he had found a better way. Entrepreneurship was appealing. The Landsman horse farm had proved that business could be lucrative if one always remembered to show a blatant disregard for the law. Business was not enough, though. His lust for money had propelled him on. The two driving forces in his life, pride and an insatiable need for money, ran on the same track, each pushing the other further and faster. His latest endeavor titillated his ego and filled his pockets. The $500,000 dividend left him reeling. He had "earned" more in several hours than most men earned in a lifetime.

Being a Dinnertime Burglar almost satisfied him, almost. Before he had even digested his success his eyes were on more. *"My own gang!"* The words sounded good. His passion was unquenchable. He could not feel good enough. Salerno had something beyond prestige and money, the thing Walter coveted most – power. Fate, Walter thought, had created *him* for power. It would necessarily be his one day. He would go far beyond Salerno. Above all, he wanted to have fear-inspiring power, the kind The Bear displayed. For this he would bide his time.

Business continued to prosper. If "earnings" were under $100,000 the jewels were fenced through a jeweler in Hallandale, Florida, named Alex Morningstar. Morningstar began his career as a small time pawn broker. As a result of his dealings with Salerno and Shaw he became the owner of two large jewelry stores. He handled as much of Salerno and Shaw's work as he possibly could but anything over $100,000 demanded a Big Apple-style jeweler.

Their New York connection, according to Walter, was Wally Gant. Gant did not need to make money fencing stolen jewelry. He dealt with Salerno because it excited him. He found pleasure by involving himself in the illegal merchandising. His fortune had come long ago when he promoted the world's first synthetic diamond, which he named the Ball de feu. This "ball-of-fire" simulation was one of the wonders of the world. People who owned expensive jewels waited in line for the opportunity to have Gant undertake a reproduction. It was Gant, says Walter, who was entrusted with the prestigious task of duplicating Elizabeth Taylor's famous jewelry. These reproductions were a lucrative trade, but tedious and hardly stimulating. Finding a market for stolen jewels kept him on his toes. Salerno delivered the jewels, and Gant payed out the cash up front. Both parties liked the arrangement. Gant, states Walter, could indulge a neurotic desire to live on the edge while Salerno could build his capital gains.

From Pennsylvania the Dinnertime Burglars headed east to Westchester County, New York. After successful visits to its finest homes they returned to Florida. In Naples, Florida, they ran into a conflict of interests. This enclave of wealth was under the jurisdiction of a crime boss out of Chicago. When he learned that the Dinnertime Burglars had set up shop right under his nose, he ordered a meeting, reproaching Salerno for working his territory uninvited. He threw down the gauntlet and demanded that they either leave or include him in the profits. Salerno rejected both alternatives and promised to leave the placid community only after he had drained it. It did not take him long.

On the Gulf of Mexico sat a one-story split-level English Tudor – style mansion. Aside from the sculptured lawns and ornate fountains, its most striking feature was its pink hue. The house was approached by a horseshoe driveway; in back it had a spacious cabana and a heartshaped swimming pool. Salerno had been tipped that the single woman who owned the home maintained an extensive jewel collection on the premises. The burglary would be handled via the Gulf of Mexico. Since the community was tightly guarded, inland roadways were precarious. The means of transportation for operations became a Zodiac motorized raft, which was small enough to be inconspicuous and portable, yet large enough to transport the men. The high-seas pirate raids might have been exciting had it not been for one terrifying detail. Walter could not swim.

With each crest he fought to hold desperate screams inside. The engine was relatively quiet, but the raft passengers had to endure a grating whine. As the waves raised and dropped the raft, the engine buzzing loud and soft, Walter felt tumultuous ragings in his stomach. A few minutes later the pontoons eased alongside a pier and Latella tied on. It was finished, half of it anyway. The return would be easier.

The three men crept up the back lawn. Latella made a wide angle around the house as Salerno pointed toward the humorous heart-shaped pool. *No more water,* Walter thought. *Not even to drink.* The pool was not amusing.

Only one light showed from the house. That was bad news. There would be no way to time the burglary. The woman was not home and might return any moment. Nevertheless, Salerno continued. As he stepped up to the darkened patio, floodlights came on. He jumped back, heart pounding, eyes reeling, and the lights went off. "It's a pressure mat, Pete," whispered Walter.

Salerno stepped up and then back down again, repeating the on-and-off lighting procedure. "I don't like it, something is not right," Salerno returned.

"It's just a pressure mat. It's activated by your foot, your weight. Go, man, get the jewels." Walter's voice broke from the dark.

"I know *that*," Salerno stated to himself. He looked the house over carefully, a house well secured and empty. His intuition told him to back off. He hesitated and then shot for the back door. Walter followed, killed the alarm that secured the house, and upon signal, Salerno pried open the door.

Once inside, another bad omen appeared before Salerno. The only way in and out of the master bedroom was a long hallway. He grunted in disgust.

Halfway down the corridor a small red laser beam stretched from its source to the other side of the wall. The beam was invisible, camouflaged by a stronger competitor – the hall light. As he strode down the corridor, he broke the red flow of energy. The interruption of light was fatal. The alarm shrieked out in pain.

Walter rushed to the raft. He pulled the chord and the engine started. Latella jumped in seconds later. "Where's Pete?" he exclaimed. They looked at each other in panic.

Salerno had not budged. He checked his watch. The police station was just two blocks away from the house. That gave the ordinary thief about five minutes to negotiate an escape. For Salerno the five minutes were a grace period to complete his job with a few seconds left for a safe departure. He ransacked each drawer and jewelry box. Jewelry crashed on top of jewelry for a full minute. The pillowcase bulged. Then Salerno dashed down the hall, out the door, and toward the raft. He squatted and threw the bag on before lowering himself in. As the craft pulled away, one of the pontoons smacked the pier, then punctured and dragged itself to annihilation. Escaping air whistled a loud warning. The raft began to sink. Walter hurled obscenities in every direction as he wildly scrambled toward the dock, nearly knocking his companions into the water. Latella cursed back and Salerno steadied the slowly sinking craft before removing the loot and tools. "We're gonna have to swim for it. The beaches will be filled with cops in a few minutes," Salerno declared.

"God, are you crazy?" said Walter.

"Calm down and get in the water," screamed Salerno over the alarm.

"No!" shouted Walter.

"Yes!" retorted Salerno.

"NOOOO!" Walter screamed.

Latella, on the verge of emotional collapse, blasted, "Freakin' guy, don't do this. We'll go to jail. Get in the water, you freakin' guy!"

"No way, NO WAY! I'm not going in the water," returned Walter.

Salerno threw up his hands in absolute frustration. *"Mama mia."* The pier erupted into hysteria, and the argument would have come to blows had it not been for the sound of sirens pulling into the driveway. The trio stood silent, not moving. Latella and Salerno could not believe that Walter would go to prison instead of *learning* to swim on the spot. Walter stared back angrily, not believing that Salerno and Latella would ask him to *drown* just to keep them out of prison. Exasperated, Salerno turned and tore down the beach. His two partners followed. Two miles later, out of breath and physically and emotionally drained, they were safe at the Holiday Inn. No one spoke.

18

CHAPTER EIGHTEEN

The next score was inspired by a sporting event. The entire gang sat leisurely watching the Bing Crosby Pebble Beach Golf Classic one Saturday afternoon. The television cameras surveyed the plush greens and fairways, the backdrop provided by the magnificent homes of Carmel-by-the-Sea. Salerno decided that afternoon that his crew deserved a working vacation.

The following Monday he withdrew $25,000 from the bank, bought four plane tickets to Los Angeles and invited Donaldson, Walter, and Dominic Latella to join him.

Pebble Beach is a seven-mile peninsula secured and guarded at its only entrance. No one, except homeowners and their guests, are allowed entry. Salerno's crew needed to study each home up close. Salerno devised the idea of posing as the representatives of a construction magnate in south Florida who had decided to move west. Before leaving Miami, Salerno had a printer make expensive business cards indicating that he was an employee of a construction company. With the impressive business cards and the necessary finesse a realtor could be duped into giving them a grand tour of the exclusive enclave.

Once in the Pebble Beach area, Salerno and his companions found a realtor who fell for their story after examining the business cards. She asked what price range interested their employer. Salerno allowed that his wealthy client looked toward one in excess of a million dollars. Such luxury, she assured him, was plentiful in the village of Carmel-by-the-Sea as well as adjoining Pebble Beach. The Dinnertime Burglars were pleased when she suggested that she not only take them into Pebble Beach but allow them to tour actual homes, a privilege not generally afforded prospective buyers. As they drove past a guard house, the realtor explained that the area was home to John Wayne, Clint Eastwood, and other famous stars, industrial moguls, and renowned professionals. (Clint Eastwood is, as of 1987, Carmel's mayor.) After the enlightening tour the four men thanked the realtor for her invaluable help.

The motel in which they were staying was about two miles from their target. When night fell the men easily penetrated the exclusive area by the beach and jumped a fence into actress Kim Novak's back lawn. One of the cardinal sins never committed by a knowledgeable burglar is to rob a home that lies between the burglary and escape. Thus Novak's home was spared, and to keep the beaches safe, the four restrained from looting all oceanfront homes. Salerno had marked a home of special interest, its owner a famous neurosurgeon. Walter admiringly pawed the Rolls-Royce that sat in the driveway with gloved hands. The job was completed without a hitch. In less than an hour the foursome were relaxing at the motel and taking inventory of the heist. Salerno pointed out that the homes in California, though more extravagant, were not as jewel-laden as those they customarily visited in Pennsylvania, New York and Florida. New wealth just did not have the time to accumulate as did the staid wealth of the East.

Walter, usually in a celebrating mood after a successful job, gazed pensively at the ocean all that night. He was unsatisfied. Carmel was fantasy-land. He had a desire to move his family to California. He would, too, he mused, were it not for the more burning desire to acquire power. Two roads lay before him. The ocean was pushing and pulling along its shore, alluring, peaceful. Walter committed once and forever. Power, he would have it.

Before returning to Miami, Salerno, Latella, Donaldson, and Shaw took a few days to enjoy the nightlife of California. One evening at an exclusive restaurant in Monterey they had finished their meal, when Dominic Latella became irritated at Walter's boisterous confidence. They had been drinking heavily. Latella insulted Walter verbally, culminating his attack by branding him a "glamorized gopher". Walter had warned the crew at the beginning of their association that if anyone, including Salerno, ever disrespected him he would retaliate violently. Every patron in the crowded restaurant heard the hollow crack of broken glass. Walter had taken an empty wine bottle and smashed it in half against the leg of his chair. He uncoiled, holding the jagged edge of the wine bottle against Latella's throat. The sharp glass rubbed against his flesh. Restaurant patrons sat stone-faced. Walter screamed, "Don't you ever disrespect me, you freaking punk. I will kill you right here. It don't mean nothing to me. I'll kill you right here and still beat the rap, you stinking bum!"

Salerno jumped up and in a conciliatory tone urged Walter to calm down. "I was . . .," Latella began.

"SHUT UP, IDIOT!" Walter blasted back. Salerno grabbed Walter, pulled him back, and held him until he put the broken bottle down. "He's not gonna do that, Pete. His life don't mean nothing to me. I'll kill him now. We ain't family."

"I know, I know, Walt... Dom, he told you not to disrespect him. Now apologize." Salerno spoke gravely. Latella, still caressing his neck, and fortunate that it was not shredded, apologized profusely.

The other diners pretended to eat as the four men left the restaurant. There was no reason to fear. The Dinnertime Burglars would be leaving southern California the next morning.

Each night Walter put in a couple of hours labor, and on those days which were not scheduled for a "big score," he and Salerno jetted to New York, turned their loot over to Wally Gant, and cashed in. Walter's takes were tremendous. He made more money than he could spend. But a burglar was not a powerbroker. He did not want to end his career as a jewel thief, but merely begin a new one. He believed he could be violent, fearless, and more manipulative than the best of the big-time crime figures he had met. All that he lacked was opportunity. One Sunday afternoon as he strolled through a dusty flea market he saw an opening, a starting place. A painting caught his eye and offered him the new role of con man extraordinaire. He was excited about the anticipated career move, although he did not fully understand that to intimidate and command respect in The Bear's world would require more than conartistry. Not even a gun would be enough. He would need a blazing gun, a gun always warm from the last time it was used.

In short, his new career would mean pain for himself and for others. Innocent people would have to pay heavy prices for his ploys. He would have to be hard, emotionless. His new line of work would demand nothing less than malicious and consistent cruelty, much more than occasional violent outbursts, such as his attack on Latella. These were the realities Walter did not fully know at the time, but when he was tested, when his resolve was questioned, he answered with a strong affirmative.

19

CHAPTER NINETEEN

There was no mistaking them. The velvet depictions of sleepy Mexican days, puppies, kittens, sombrero-wearing children, lions, tigers, and nudes too, drew curious glances from customers at flea markets, bus stations, and road-side stands. In the fall of 1971 they were making an impressive, albeit tasteless, debut into the marketplace. People became passionate with their affection for the velvet paintings. Sales soared. An Atlanta-based corporation, Doyle Original Arts, produced them. Walter had seen them in the flea markets on occasion. He was not particularly interested in the works themselves (his Day-Glow pink, maroon, and blue silk suits more than filled his craving for the outlandish and gaudy); however, he was fascinated with the sales they were racking up. The paintings made money, and where money was concerned, Walter was concerned. The one redeeming feature of Doyle's original velvet tacky paintings was their ability to generate cash. This fact struck a chord of culture in Walter Thiel Shaw, Jr., and motivated him to become an art collector.

The enthusiastic art-patron-to-be called Atlanta requesting

information on distributorships. Tim Ernst and John Ashley, two sales representatives from Doyle, agreed to drive down and discuss a distributorship for south Florida.

For their dinner meeting, Walter wore his sharpest Peter Kent suit. His smile was as radiant as his jewelry. The sales representatives were impressed. Walter droned a slow seduction which was irresistible to the Georgians. He prophesied that he would make them very wealthy; led them to believe that he owned several multi-million dollar operations ;chuckled as he stated that he was always looking for more money, but not more taxes; engrossed them with his brilliant idea to form a new company for the distribution of paintings; applauded them for their expertise; fascinated them with a business plan which placed Tim Ernst as the corporation's president, John Ashley as vice-president and Bonnie Shaw as secretary-treasurer; inflated their egos by assuring them that with their ten years experience working for Doyle they could easily provide the new corporation a line of credit; dazzled them with a guarantee of $25,000 up front if they would grant him a line of credit for the balances; stunned them by asking for 10,000 paintings; and ultimately; lured them into a ruthless, relentless and flawless con.

Both men explained that Doyle, the owner of the company, would not readily agree to release 10,000 paintings on credit. Walter felt confident he would. "Remember, I'm making you part of the corporation. You arrange for me to get the paintings on credit, and not only will you receive a commission on them, but a percentage of the corporation's profits. We'll make a killing."

Later, at Walter's house, Ernst called Doyle and presented him with the deal. Doyle expressed reservations, but Ernst doggedly assured him that the new client was trustworthy. "He's a millionaire. I've met his wife and kids. I've seen his house. Believe me on this one. I've worked for you for ten years, and you know I'm a good judge of character. This guy can move product." He hung up the phone telling the others the good news – Doyle agreed to the terms. Walter recalls that Ernst managed only a half-smile. He could not relax. If the deal was so good, why did he have a gnawing twitch in the pit of his stomach? If Walter failed, it would mean his job. Doyle had promised to terminate both of them if they stumbled, even though they had been loyal to him for ten years. The cost was enormous, at ten dollars a painting the entire company could totter and possibly fold if the deal turned sour.

The next day Walter drove the men to a warehouse. On the front hung a large sign that read: "Foreign Trading Corporation." Walter had had it made a few days earlier. Foreign Trading Corporation did not have a legal existence. It was a part of the elaborate scam. The warehouse itself had been rented. Walter boasted that it was one of several he owned.

He told Ernst and Ashley that a bank account would be opened under their names along with Bonnie's. For tax purposes, he explained, he did not want to go on the account or own a percentage of the business. Also for tax reasons, he would sublet space in the warehouse to them as president and vice-president of the company as well as his wife as secretary-treasurer. As Ernst and Ashley were leaving to return to Atlanta, Walter had them sign checks for a Panasonic televised electronic surveillance system, carpentry work, and three months' rent at $620 a month, all amounting to about $5,000. The men signed believing that Walter had the money in the bank ready to be transferred to the new account. If not, why would he put his wife's name on the checking account? As long as she was liable, they were safe. Walter handed John an envelope containing a cashier's check for $25,000 as if it were an old newspaper clipping. Ernst and Ashley took note of his ease. Ernst examined the check and buckled. The check was not endorsed. "No problem," said Walter confidently, "my investor just forgot to sign it. I'll give it to you when you come back with the paintings." Anxious to get back home, Ernst agreed. After all, not even a dumb cluck would put his wife on the line if he were playing games.

Walter passed the checks, signed by Ernst and Ashley, on to carpenters and a Panasonic dealer without placing funds in the account. When John Ashley returned with a truckload of 5,000 paintings, Walter helped the hired laborers unload the truck. After emptying it, Ashley turned to his new business partner with an exuberant smile. "All set!"

"Not quite," replied Walter. Ashley followed him into the warehouse to receive the worst news he had heard since grade school, when he learned that General Robert E. Lee had, in fact, surrendered to General Grant at Appomattox.

Walter pulled off his jacket, revealing two newly purchased Browning .9-millimeter pistols. He carefully hung the jacket over a chair. The party was over. His voice was soft. Ashley, he explained, was responsible for $5,000 in bad checks. Walter continued, "Here in Florida passing bad checks is a felony about like Murder One. A bad check is straight jail time, no questions asked."

Ashley broke into tears. He had a family. He had a good life back in Atlanta. Walter assured him that possibly there was a way out. All he would have to do was never show his face in Florida or Georgia again. Walter promised to handle the bad checks and give him $1,500 in cash to help with the move. "It's that, or five to ten, you decide," said Walter.

Ashley peered out of strained eyes. It was difficult to think with a gun-carrying maniac pressing him. "Yes, yes, God, whatever you say. Just don't let me go to jail."

"That's it, good thinking," Shaw reassured him. As Ashley

drove back to Georgia for the last time, he knew Doyle Original Arts was finished. It would be difficult to cover the loss. The entire corporation would go down at the hands of a twenty-one-year-old con man.

Before Ashley arrived in Atlanta, Ernst had left for Miami with his 5,000 paintings. Shaw gave him the same prognosis and prescription, and though he was as sick as his partner, Ernst refused to take the bitter medicine. He stormed out of the warehouse to the nearest phone booth to alert the Pembrook Pines Police Department. He returned to the warehouse when the officers arrived, demanding that the 5,000 paintings be reloaded onto his truck and that Walter be arrested for fraud. Shaw explained that he did not know what the "irate gentlemen" was talking about. He did know, however, that Mr. Ernst had written him three bad checks totaling $1,860 in payment for warehouse space.

Amid Tim Ernst's protests, Walter showed the officers the three $620 bounced checks. "I'm sorry, Mr. Ernst, but we can't recover your merchandise until you reimburse Mr. Shaw," one of the officers said.

Ernst exploded, "What! This man is a fraud. I just delivered the product. He ripped me off . . ."

"There's nothing we can do, Mr. Ernst," interrupted the officer.

As the squad car pulled away, Ernst, still livid, stared at Walter, threatening to beat him. Left with no other choice, Walter removed his jacket, revealing the deadly pistols again. Ernst ran to his car shouting obscenities.

Walter started selling the paintings immediately. A flea market hood nicknamed Vic Dante stole five of the best nudes in the collection. Walter demanded payment for the vulgar works. The towering Dante refused. When Walter informed Dante that he was under The Bear's protection, Vic Dante made the mistake of demanding proof.

The Bear showed up at the flea market one night, quietly strolled over to Dante, seized his arm, and snapped it with an effortless twist. The frightened giant knelt before The Bear, nursing his broken limb. "If I have to come down here again, it will be your life. Now pay Walt his money." The Bear smiled, nodded greetings to nearby shoppers, and walked out. Vic Dante reached into his pocket with his good arm and humbly offered to pay Walter.

The Dante episode was hardly more than a minor nuisance, but the next difficulty was more troubling. Doyle sued Bonnie for fraud. As an officer of the corporation, she was liable. Walter hired attorney Bro Hinckley to defend her. In turn, Hinckley persuaded Doyle to settle for ten cents on the dollar. Walter states that after one payment the attorney instructed her to stop. Doyle was foiled. Agreeing to settle on his claim, he had placed the case in civil court and would have difficulties filing criminal charges. Before the civil case could proceed to trial the paintings were gone.

It was a sweet deal. After expenses, Walter netted a clean $210,000. His gain nearly bankrupted Doyle Original Arts. Doyle was fighting for his last shirt and tie and swore that he would take Shaw down. But for Shaw, business was good, very good. He was great, possibly the best.

20

CHAPTER TWENTY

The burglary business required fresh infusions of blood from time to time. To keep the supply flowing, Salerno would take out a rookie. Such occasions were dangerous, and in retrospect hilarious, given that the new man never failed to bumble into a personal disaster. Salerno told one rookie that he was too big and clumsy to be a good burglar – "a big salami."

The kid persisted. On the first night out, after Salerno's warning never to run from a house (due to the possibility of hitting trees, snagging clotheslines, or dropping into swimming pools), the kid shot out like a full-throttled jet the minute he was spooked. Salerno and Shaw watched him run across the lawn in the moonlight, feet flying, until suddenly he disappeared. The rookie had vanished. Walter turned to Salerno, "Did you just see what I saw?" Walter tried to fathom the meaning of the miraculous event that had just occurred. A man had dissolved into nothingness right before his eyes. Then it dawned on the two masters. The "big salami" had not disappeared, he had fallen. They walked out and focused their penlights into the deep end of a drained swimming pool. There, lying face down, oblivious to the realm of consciousness, was the rookie.

"Like a big salami!" Salerno repeated. They dragged him out. Groaning and sprawled out on the pool deck, he peered deeply into Walter's eyes and asked two of life's most pressing questions, "Who am I?" followed by "Why am I here?"

Another amateur ventured out with the Dinnertime Boys one snowy January night during a visit to the Northeast. He was forewarned. "The mountains are dangerous. Don't wander around."

Once on the job he boasted that his Vietnam training had equipped him to handle mountain terrain better than either Shaw or Salerno. "I've been to Vietnam. I know my way around mountain territory, I . . . ahh ahhh!" He never finished the sentence. In the next few seconds the peaceful mountain air was alive with howling, screaming, and the sounds of a thousand snapping tree limbs. The rookie had walked off the side of a mountain.

In the high-pressure world of jewel theft, errors were not the sole prerogative of rookies. Dominic Latella held an unofficial record for goofs. He kept his job, in spite of blunders, because he was Salerno's relative. Although he had been out many times, neither his bladder nor his bowels could tolerate the tension, and each time he ran through the woods to escape angry homeowners, vicious dogs, or pursuing police, dandy Dominic lost control, defecating and urinating all over himself. He would run along pleading, "I gotta stop. Please, I gotta stop. I'm going in my pants."

Shaw always replied, "You stop and you're busted." Finally the problem became so habitual that Latella included toilet paper in his burglary arsenal.

Even the masters slipped up. During one burglary, Shaw and Salerno were confronted with a collection of taxidermy in a house large enough to be a wildlife preserve. The game room was cluttered with the bodily remains of exotic animals collected from around the globe. The lions, tigers, and bears formed a chilling panoramic view and the dimly lit room possessed a spirit all its own.

The two jewel thieves looked over their situation nervously. Walter commented that the animals seemed angry. Salerno chuckled uneasily. Intellectually, they understood and accepted that a dead, mounted bear or panther was incapable of attacking, but the knowledge did not translate to their nervous systems. Walter's wide eyes met the glowing, glassy stare of each animal. Salerno whispered, "Weird, man."

"Let's get out of here," Walter said.

"Master bedroom first." Salerno, ever the professional, had to complete the job.

They backed out of the room and crept down the hall. Walter's mind flashed reel after reel of bears and tigers ripping human carcasses to pieces. In the master bedroom, Salerno noticed a large hanging birdcage with a cloth draped over it. He tapped Walter and pointed toward it. "It's probably alive," Walter said suspiciously.

"It's probably a bird," Salerno teased. The cage hung over the dresser. To collect valuables the men had to work underneath it. Walter quickly searched each drawer and filled his pillowcase, cocking his head at an angle to keep an eye on the dangling cage. When the drawers were sacked, Walter backed off, leaving Salerno to continue.

A few seconds later he stepped toward the cage. Curiosity had conquered fear. He tried to remind himself, "It's a bird – no big deal." But he was unconvinced. The game room had been occupied by an angry herd of carnivores. Who could guess what hid beneath the cloth covering of the cage? Walter slowly lifted the cloth to peek into the cage.

Before his eyes had focused, before the penlight had penetrated the darkness, there came an explosion of sound more intense than any alarm. "Hoo, Hoo, Hoo!" It was the loudest series of noises Walter had ever heard. Instantly he rocketed across the room. Salerno, whose impromptu escape effort had caused him to smack face-first into a bedroom wall, fell to the carpet.

"What the hell?" Shaw whispered emphatically.

"It's a damn owl," answered Salerno. "What were you doing, Shaw?"

"What do you mean, what was I doing? That damn owl nearly caused me a heart attack. What are you doing on the floor?" Shaw shot back. The Dinnertime Burglars grabbed their score and ran down the hallway, past the game room, and out to freedom.

In 1973 the gang moved their act to Connecticut for the first time. One stately mansion was so jewel-laden that three pillowcases were employed in an effort to make a thorough collection. Before Shaw and Salerno had finished their heist, they heard the distinct sound of footsteps in the hall approaching the master bedroom. They darted behind the door just as the lady of the house entered the bedroom to see her jewelry scattered across the dresser. Pete turned his head to Shaw's ear. "We can't let her out of this room, she knows we're here." Shaw breathed heavily. This was worse than the owl escapade. This was worse than anything.

Following Salerno's command he shut the door. The lady turned and let out an uninhibited, undignified, old-fashioned bloodcurdling scream. She followed the first with an even better performance. And then another. Finally, although she had probably lived in the old house for years and was well acquainted with the locations of the doors, she began to run full-speed into every wall in the room. She bounced frantically from wall to wall, trying, possibly, to make an exit. "Walt, I can't believe what I'm seeing. Is she doing what I see her doing?" Salerno asked.

Walter tried to assure her that they meant her no bodily harm. The message was ineffective. The more they pleaded for her to relax, the wilder the display. Hitting one wall too many, and defeated, she slumped to the floor and began urinating in her clothes. Half-dazed, Walter opened the door to see the butler running up the stairway. Salerno grabbed a huge vase and tossed it at him. Unable to resist a good game of catch, the butler made a valiant attempt to participate, but the heavy vase toppled him. He crashed down the winding staircase. In the ballroom below, inebriated guests jerked in disbelief. Salerno grabbed his twelve-inch pry bar and yelled, "Charge!" The two intruders parted the sea of people and ran out the front door.

The next morning Walter walked from his hotel room to the lobby to get a newspaper. The headline said: "Six-Foot Giants Charge Party with Sabers." "I could swear that neither one of us is over five-ten, or five-eleven," he told Salerno when he returned to the room.

21

CHAPTER TWENTY-ONE

When Walter was not out of state or on a score, he was sharpening his skill for inflicting pain. Bursting at the seams with energy, he never tired of his occupation, never needed rest. His million-dollar burglaries were dinnertime activities. For lunch he had a taste for extortion and intimidation.

In 1972, he accompanied Tony Plate, a feared underboss in the Gambino family, to a car lot. The owner of the lot, Sid Carp, had borrowed money from Plate and reneged on paying it back. Carp responded to Plate's threatening collection tactics by turning him into the Feds. Plate posted bond and paid Carp an immediate visit. He asked Walter to join him. The two walked into Carp's office. Walter locked the door. The troubled man sprang from his desk chair. Walter knocked him back down. Next, the Gambino family underboss gave Carp a brutal warning, after which Shaw lunged over the desk and sunk his teeth into Carp's face, tearing a chunk of flesh from his cheek. He shook his head like a rabid wolf and spewed the human meat back into Carp's face. For this rare performance, one that was admired in hangouts all over Miami, Shaw received a brand-new Cadillac Eldorado. His reputation was growing. He was a comer to watch.

In 1973 a jewelry store owner switched a diamond on one of Walter's friends. When the new diamond turned out to be synthetic, Walter decided to "push" the jeweler. He visited the store to explain to the jeweler that he had come to have his friend's diamond replaced. The store owner began to boast of a .25 automatic, which he kept in the back of his store, and how he had always had an itch to use it to "clean up scum."

Undaunted, Walter convinced the owner to walk out to the parking lot. The two approached an ominous black Lincoln. Inside it sat one of Walter's henchmen, the jewelry store owner's ex-wife, and his three-year-old son. Walter explained that he would chop the boy into little pieces and send them to the jeweler COD if he did not cooperate. The owner cooperated.

The benefits derived from unbridled brutality seemed unlimited. Few, Walter thought, had the guts, talent, or brains for it. If he could cultivate it, develop it, demonstrate it at appropriate times, without conscience or second thoughts, he could write his own ticket. But brutality had to be coupled with smarts. Impulsive brutality led nowhere. It had to be directed and purposeful. Observing The Bear had taught him this. Those violent goons on the street who were brutal just for the sake of brutality, never got anywhere.

From The Bear he was learning another valuable lesson, that is, appreciating his cash flow by starting legitimate businesses that also served as fronts for illegitimate endeavors. His first venture was a clothing store. He acquired the store he would later name The Apple Boutique through a cruel betrayal in 1970.

Howard Wieselberg owned a successful men's clothing store. Walter wanted it. He had tried to interest the wealthy young man in an assortment of vices – drugs, women, anything to get a foot in the door for blackmail. After numerous unsuccessful attempts, he pinpointed Wieselberg's vulnerability. He was a homosexual. Walter visited the store and tried on pants several sizes too small. Wieselberg was tantalized by the sizing mistakes. Wieselberg's appetite was whetted. Walter informed him that he was with the Mafia and had been doing his best to protect the store from an outright takeover. Wieselberg thought Walter's overtures were more than platonic, a view that Walter deliberately encouraged. Walter produced a ridiculous story: "Your store is being targeted by mobsters. They want it. Now if they see I'm involved, they'll back off."

Wieselberg flirtatiously surrendered stock to Walter, not much, but enough to keep him around. The young man thought he was giving chase, when in fact he was being hunted. Walter played the abhorrent part well, and within a few months, he owned nearly fifty percent of the small outlet. When he demanded more, Wieselberg asked for more too. "I love you, Walter. I want us to be together. I'll give you anything, just don't leave me . . ."

Walter nearly faltered; the game was becoming grotesque. He almost felt sorry for Wieselberg, but he would not let up. In the final analysis he couldn't have cared less if the young "queer" committed suicide over the developing trauma. Pity was for the pitiable. Walter was a warrior. He promised Wieselberg, "I'll never leave you, you know that, but if you really love me, you'll give me the store, let me take care of it for you – I'll protect you."

The store was signed over to Walter, and he, in turn, had Wieselberg order several thousand dollars worth of new merchandise. The store lacked the financial strength for such a large order, so Wieselberg signed personal guarantees. When the bill came due, Walter refused to pay. Since Wieselberg's name was on the invoice as personal guarantor, he was liable. Walter, as the new owner, was not.

While Walter converted the store into a ladies' boutique, Wieselberg, under the threat of expensive court battles and with heart torn asunder, checked into a psychiatric clinic. Four years later he showed up on Walter's doorstep – broke, broken, and disillusioned. Walter was not home, but Bonnie invited him in. He told of his four years of hell, of his poverty, and finally of how he had lost his health, wealth, and mental well-being over an unrequited love. Bonnie, revolted, ordered him to leave and never come back. As she slammed the door in his face, he began to explain that he had not come for money or revenge. Nor had he come to lay guilt at Walter's feet for completely ruining his life. He had come merely to tell Walter . . . he still loved him.

Wieselberg's store became the Apple Boutique and Walter smiled wryly every time he thought of the tortuous chain of events that led to its acquisition. He visited his stores often. (A second clothing store, Archie's Pants, was purchased outright.) They were flattering reminders of his success. He kept in close contact with The Bear and Tom Palmer. The latter had come to be a source of protection through Salerno. Palmer, of Murder Inc., fame, was a home-grown mafioso. This Italian boss used "Tom Palmer" as a pseudonym; his Sicilian name was Tony Greco. Greco, at that time, was one of the most feared mobsters in the Southeast, and Walter was fortunate to have been counted as a friend. As a member of the infamous La Cosa Nostra, this powerful and impatient man was not to be toyed with. Neither Palmer nor Salerno, however, suspected that Walter was under the watchful supervision of The Bear. This little secret gave Walter a decided edge over Salerno, although Salerno did not know it.

With each day Walter's bold, flashy, and often maniacal behavior widened a chasm between him and his companions. When Walter took John Donaldson's advice and exchanged his .38 special for the two Browning .9 millimeters, Salerno grew leery. Shaw never left the house without both guns strapped to his sides. Salerno did not carry a gun. Long ago he had known violence, but, as his material status grew, he put away his weapons, as "childish ways," and concentrated on enjoying life's many splendors. He was still the best burglar alive, but he had grown soft. Violence was unnecessary and vulgar. Apparently he had taken on the philosophy and mannerisms of those from whom he had stolen for so long.

Walter had amassed considerable wealth too. He had reached millionaire status, tax-free. He lived in an elegant marble-floored home adjoining the golf course of one of Hollywood, Florida's exclusive developments. He owned some forty pairs of expensive shoes to match a wardrobe worth tens of thousands of dollars, and he had purchased one exotic automobile after another for himself and Bonnie. His fingers were bedecked with expensive jewelry. He exposed himself to every imaginable luxury. Still, the effect of it all, simply did not satisfy him. These were merely symbols pointing to his success, a fodder for more glory. Unpredictable behavior, fearlessness and an increasing bent toward violence began to trouble those around him. In their world, power was not an independent entity. It was always wielded by someone, and to gain it meant wresting it from its owner. Walter was waiting for the wrong place and the wrong time.

22

CHAPTER TWENTY-TWO

After buying Archie's Pants and seizing the store that became the Apple Boutique, Walter made a move on a south Florida excavating company called Global Excavating. Jimmy Myers, owner of the company, had come to Walter for money. Walter agreed to make the loan if Myers would put up corporate stock as security. Myers agreed, but instead of receiving the promised cash from Walter, he received a promissory note for $50,000. Weeks passed and Walter did not make good on the note. When bill collectors threatened Myers with lawsuits, he was ready for Walter's new offer. "Jimmy, I'll take care of the bills if you pay my weekly protection fee. Two advantages, my friend. One, you'll never get fired. I don't do business like that. And secondly, this kind of thing will never happen to you again."

Myers protested, "But you lied to me. If you had given me the $50,000, I wouldn't need you now. Hey, man, I gave you the stock. How can you do this? You're sick."

"No, you misunderstood me, Jimmy. I'm here to help you. But the choice is yours, unemployment or a successful career under new management. You've got five minutes to decide."

Myers didn't need the five minutes. With a family to feed, he met Walter's terms. Walter took the company and began draining it. He gave Salerno a $300 weekly salary, took $300 himself, and provided Salerno's father-in-law, John Savino, with $500 a week. The men did not need the money, but they needed the front. Every front helped. Myers dutifully accepted his subordinate position. Perhaps their working relationship would have continued unimpeded had it not been for the Dinner time rivalry.

Salerno was jealous. He was fading while Walter took on stronger pigments. One evening Salerno and his father-in-law paid Jimmy Myers a visit. Salerno's story was simple. He told Jimmy that he was much more powerful than Walter and had been all along. He explained that Tom Palmer was Walter's source of power and that it was he, Salerno, who had introduced Walter to Palmer in the first place. "I knew Palmer before Walter could pick his nose. The only reason Palmer protects him is because I asked him to, as a favor to me. Shaw's a nobody."

Salerno also informed Myers that he had decided to take up the protective reins of Global Excavating. Myers was confused. Who was he to believe? He was just a businessman. He had worked hard for his company until Shaw came along. Now he was being told to give it to yet another hood. When Salerno left, he called Walter. Walter pounded his fist down on the kitchen counter. Immediately, the very second he heard the story, he burst into an angry sweat.

"Walter, I'm just in the middle. Don't get angry with me. I mean, what am I supposed to do? I've got a family," Myers explained.

Walter flared back. "Shut up. You want to know what to do. Tell Salerno to go to hell. I don't get my power from Palmer. I get my power from someone I was with a year before I ever met Salerno, and God help Pete 'cause this guy is gonna take him and Palmer both and rip their lungs out of their freakin' throats. Stay alive, Jimmy. Tell Salerno to get lost."

Myers was innocent in the takeover attempt. Walter knew this, but he did not care. If it felt good to rip Myers, he'd rip him. If it felt good to *kill* Myers, he'd do that too, and in this case, if Myers, though innocent, had to be destroyed, so be it.

Walter telephoned The Bear and related Salerno's move to him. The Bear growled. Next, Walter called Salerno and told him that there would be a sit-down over his latest stunt. "Well, Walter, I've got Palmer backing me up on this a hundred percent. The sit-down's a mere formality. Just what made you think Palmer would protect you over me, anyway?" Salerno responded confidently.

Walter shot back. "Pete, the sit-down ain't with Palmer. It's with an old friend I knew long before you."

"Yeah, who's he connected to?" asked Salerno.

"That's the beauty. He ain't connected to nobody, baby." Shaw laughed.

"Smart, Shaw, you just bought yourself and your lovely friend a ticket to hell. Palmer is gonna crack your skull, and when he finds out you pitted this idiot against him, the guy's gonna take a fall too," boomed Salerno.

"Be at the Howard Johnson's on I-95 and Hollywood Boulevard tonight at eight, wise guy." Shaw slammed down the receiver.

Salerno and his father-in-law, arrived at ten after eight, laughing and boisterous. They saw a heavyset, muscular man sitting in a booth, staring into space indifferently. Salerno walked over and asked him if he was Walter's friend. "I've taken care of Walter since he was nineteen, just a baby . . . Sit down."

Salerno's eyes were caught by The Bear's. His jovial mood evaporated. Shaw never learned from The Bear or Salerno exactly what was said that night. He only gleaned a few details. Salerno and Savino left the restaurant in a pool of sweat and rushed to apologize profusely to Myers and Walter, assuring the two that he and his associate were backing off forever. Walter could show them all the disrespect he desired. The Bear had made them believers. Salerno never looked Shaw in the eyes again. He never mentioned Palmer. He obeyed. The Bear had gained his obedience for a lifetime. He had never been more frightened than he was at the Howard Johnson's sit-down. He had Palmer, but what good did it do? He wondered what good anyone could do, even God.

As he later allowed, in The Bear he had confronted indescribable power, an atomic bomb that might explode at any minute, blowing him straight to kingdom come. The thought of leaving behind bank accounts and his lovely home was downright troubling. Each time he thought about The Bear, for days constantly, he saw himself at Howard Johnsons, staring defiantly into The Bear's dark eyes, listening, disbelieving, then believing, and finally believing unconditionally. He could see his head drop and his skin pale. The excruciating experience played back in slow motion. *That voice, that low grating voice. The sinking feeling, in too deep, in too deep. I need help. God, this is a nightmare. Let me go.*

Then he was let go and he was thankful for the grace period The Bear had allowed him. He was alive, that was enough. He could regroup later, perhaps slow down too. Time might allow him to regain his confidence, though he doubted it. And he loathed Walter. The young, conceited glory-hog had won again. He seemed to be always acting tough, always playing a part. Salerno wanted to kill him, but that would never come to fruition. The Bear had spoken, and every time he passed the bright orange shingles of a Howard Johnson's he shivered and paid homage to a new temple and a jealous new god. One wrong move and the god would demand a sacrifice, a human sacrifice.

23

CHAPTER TWENTY-THREE

Doyle had been in a long, protracted fight to save his corporation after Walter's swindle. This done, he could concentrate on a more enjoyable task – revenge. Convinced that he could not retrieve his monetary losses, he moved for a death penalty and hired a Mafia soldier from the Funzi Terra family. Johnny "Potatoes" was attempting to earn a reputation as a killer. When hired, he in turn enlisted the support of three other "torpedoes" (hit men) to terminate Walter.

The four men arrived in Miami and drove directly to Walter's house. Bonnie explained that her husband had left for the day on business. When Johnny Potatoes insisted that it was urgent that he contact Walter Thiel, a tremor of fear shook Bonnie. The only people who knew the name Thiel were those within the family, the Mafia family. She excused herself and called Walter at Archie's Pants. Walter tried to calm her, but her fears were justified. He began to fidget nervously. "Bonnie, just calm down and put one of them on the phone. No, wait . . . yeah, put one of them on the phone."

Johnny Potatoes told Walter that he had come to deliver an

urgent message. Walter did not recognize his voice. The visit could not be friendly. "Well, I'm busy so go ahead and give me the message," replied Walter.

"Not over the phone, it's too important," came the response. A meeting was arranged for 10:00 that night at a Denny's restaurant next to the Pembrook Pines Shopping Mall. Putting the receiver down, Walter turned to Donaldson. Walter had made an excellent decision in hiring the six-foot-three, 280-pound Donaldson as his bodyguard and driver. His hulking friend, however, did not provide solace concerning the ominous call. Walter telephoned the Hollandale Police Department promising them that an interesting party would be held at 10:00 in Denny's parking lot if they wished to attend.

He put the receiver down and began to search for answers. Who in the world, who in the family, who would be looking for him? The timing was wrong, the situation unacceptable. Walter was the hunter, not the prey. He could not swallow his new role. Donaldson tried to calm him. It was no use. He unwound and in so doing he became strong, wild-strong and confident. This was an opportunity to unleash hostilities, a chance to take somebody's head off. He stewed all day, allowing his anger to fester. Then at 9:00, he and Donaldson left for the meeting.

Donaldson packed a gun in a plastic store bag and stood beside a vacant car twenty yards from Walter, who leaned against his blue Cadillac. A few minutes before ten, a long, chocolate-brown Continental pulled up beside him. Rushing toward it, Walter grabbed the door handle on the driver's side and forced it open. Johnny Potatoes was caught off guard. Before he could speak Walter told him that he was being covered. Johnny Potatoes looked back. Donaldson took a sarcastic bow. Johnny got out of the car, and nervously motioned for Walter to follow him to the rear of the

Continental. He tapped the trunk a few times poetically and waited, almost embarrassed. Walter backed off. Something weird, even for a late-night rendezvous with strangers, was taking place. "Let's go inside before we attract a crowd," Walter suggested.

Before Walter and Donaldson entered Denny's they disarmed themselves, leaving the Brownings under the front seat. The police would be on hand. As the four men sat down, Johnny and his partner nudged into Donaldson and Walter. Walter reared back as if to strike and the men apologized. The contact was to determine if Walter and Donaldson were armed. Nothing but ribs – Johnny Potatoes breathed easier. Walter, too keyed-up to notice the subtle check, began the conversation.

"I know who you are . . . Surprise. I have an inside man and I ran a check on you down at the police station. It's as simple as this. I don't want to talk to you."

Johnny leaned back and released a steady stream of air between his lips. "Who are you connected to?" he asked finally.

That was it. Walter understood now. He wouldn't have needed that information if he were not going to make a hit. Johnny Potatoes had come to make a hit, but he didn't want to step on anyone's toes. The solution was easy enough. His life was secure. He could answer that he was with Tom Palmer, and the visitors would leave empty-handed. Better yet, The Bear. Either way he was safe. But did he want safety? Who was this fool? Did he really think he could take the life of one as deadly as Walter Thiel Shaw? This was an opportunity to demonstrate power. He would command respect. "You see my hand, Johnny? Well, my hand is connected to my wrist, and my wrist is connected to my arm, and so forth and so on, but what you're talking about, baby, I ain't connected to nobody." Few past experiences had offered Walter so much to savor. Johnny was annoyed. When he asked his question again, only to get the same response, he stormed out of the restaurant. Walter sat laughing.

Johnny Potatoes approached a parking lot security guard and asked for a light. He engaged the guard in a conversation, raising his arms up and down as if to indicate the dialogue was heated. Obviously, he wished to lure Walter into thinking that he was having trouble with the guard. That would convince Walter that the hit was off. Walter was high on himself, exuberant and ready for anything. When he saw what appeared to be an argument in the parking lot, his enthusiasm carried him out of the restaurant. "What seems to be the problem, gentlemen?" he interrupted with an enormous smile.

In the next second he felt the barrel of a gun in his ribs. Johnny's partner had moved behind, getting the drop on him. Walter froze. After the security guard passed to the other side of the parking lot, Johnny gave a last command. "Tell me who you're connected to before I kill you, Shaw."

Donaldson, who had stood silently, uncoiled a vicious right hook, knocking Johnny's partner off Walter. The gun fell from his grip, and Donaldson grabbed it.

Walter resumed his stage performance. "You want to know who I'm connected with, hotshot? Now that I could blow your head off, I think I'll tell you. Does the name Tom Palmer ring a bell?"

Johnny's eyes rolled and he cursed. Palmer was powerful, much too powerful for him. He looked at Walter. Paralyzed with fear, he could still hate, and he hated Walter for allowing him to jeopardize his life. To threaten the life of someone "protected" was paramount to losing life. Johnny Potatoes' career was about to end. Walter let out a rude laugh; Johnny walked toward his car. As Johnny and his men drove from the parking lot, a police car cut in front of them. They were dragged out of the car. Shaw, Donaldson, Johnny, and his partner were arrested. The four men looked at each other. What was going on?

"Over here, look what we've got here," shouted one of the officers. Face up in the trunk of Johnny's chocolate-brown Continental lay a very frustrated man. In one sweaty hand he clutched a .12-gauge sawed-off high standard shotgun, and in the other hand a .32-caliber revolver. "What were ya huntin' in there?" one policeman asked chuckling.

Walter knew exactly what he was hunting. "You s.o.b.," he whispered in Johnny's direction.

A front-page feature article on Walter Shaw in the *Miami Herald* (Oct. 26, 1975) carried these comments from Detective Tranfa, one of the arresting officers. "There was a man inside the trunk of their Lincoln Continental with a .12-gauge high standard shotgun and a .32-caliber revolver. Apparently the men were supposed to lure Shaw over to the car, the man would jump out of the trunk and shoot him . . . But the trunk locked on him, and he had trouble breathing, so he started thumping. Customers heard and called the Hollandale office, which relayed the information to us. We called for a marked car, and when it came, the men in the Lincoln pulled off. The car stopped them, opened the trunk and found the man with the shotgun. We questioned them (the three men), Shaw and Donaldson, from 11 to 6 A.M., but it was like talking to a wall. They were right out of Humphrey Bogart."

When the men were finally released, Walter learned that Johnny Potatoes had ordered a fourth accomplice to hold Bonnie and their two children at gunpoint and to await further orders. The import of the plot thickened. The Mafia posted a strict standard of do's and don'ts, laws that were rigidly enforced.

Johnny Potatoes and his three "goons" had broken two important rules. They had tried to kill Walter, who was under

Palmer's protection. Attempting a hit without Palmer's express consent showed contempt for the "law." To disrespect a boss could carry a death penalty. Second, they were prepared to kill Walter's wife and children, a definite taboo.

Palmer, informed of the fiasco, called a sit-down. Pete Salerno and Donaldson attended. Walter was sent out of town. He returned to a bloodfest. Johnny Potatoes had been pardoned with a reprimand only because of his ties to the Funzi Tierra family.

The others, unfortunately, lacked any protection. They were discovered by police in a field outside of Miami – hands tied behind their backs, kneeling as if to pray or more probably beg mercy, with three bulletholes in each man's head. Whether the brutal killings were directly related to impropriety involving Shaw is unclear. What was clear, the men were dead.

24

CHAPTER TWENTY-FOUR

Walter and Bonnie spent New Year's Eve of 1972 with a well-known nightclub singer, Mickey Finn, and his girlfriend, Sybil, who was Bonnie's sister. After dinner the couples headed for the Thunderbird Hotel, where Miami, Beach's hottest night spot was located. The Thunderbird's famous club was packed with Dionysian pleasure-seekers, each trying to reach an all-time high in intoxication before the new year began. Bonnie and Sybil excused themselves from the table to freshenup as Walter ordered another round of drinks. It was difficult to hear above the revelry. The alcohol, mixed with a driving beat, entranced partygoers into a buzzing half consciousness. Walter stared at Mickey through swollen slits, unable to understand what his friend was saying. Suddenly, through the noise, he heard Mickey mention The Bear. He leaned across the table to hear the story. Much of it was unintelligible, blurred through Mickey's slurred speech and the incessant noise. But one important piece of information drilled into his skull. *The Bear had made a pass at Bonnie.*

Walter's hands knotted into fists. When Bonnie

approached the table, he jumped up and seized her arm. She tried to break away, but Walter herded her out of the club.

"Why didn't you tell me?" Walter stormed.

"Tell you what? Let go of my arm, you're hurting me," she responded.

"Don't play with me, Bonnie. Did The Bear ask you out or not?"

Walter's question was as unsettling as the experience that precipitated it. She burst into tears and pleaded with Walter to calm down.

"I've already told your father. He said he would take care of it. Walter, it was nothing. I told him off, and it was forgotten. Please, baby, just let it alone. He could kill you. He didn't touch me, but he'll kill you."

Walter wanted the whole story, down to the last detail. A few weeks earlier Walter and Bonnie attended a party thrown by The Bear. While Walter drank and laughed with the boys, Bonnie had gone into the game room to play billiards. Minutes later The Bear joined her. During the course of play, a billiard ball lodged in one of the pockets. Bonnie freed it, saying, "It's coming down."

The Bear responded, "It sure is."

Next he asked her if she had heard an old Frank Sinatra tune called "When and Where."

Bonnie stated that Frank Sinatra had never, to her knowledge, recorded a song called "When and Where."

Crack – The Bear made an explosive break. "You know, honey, it goes like this: 'when are we going out and where will we meet?'" ... *Crack* – the nine ball slammed down into the corner pocket below Bonnie's navel. As she jumped back her eyes met The Bear's.

"How can you do that? Walter looks up to you, he loves you," she lectured.

The Bear dropped the pool stick on the table and walked toward her. Then he stopped.

"I just wanted to see if you were loyal to the kid. He doesn't even have to know about this. I was just looking out for him," he said.

"No – no you weren't. I can't believe you would do this. He looks up to you," she said, backing away.

The Bear picked up the pool stick again and drove the three ball hard, but it steered off its trajectory.

"Who's gonna tell? I won't." He looked up. "It's your turn." Bonnie had left the room.

Listening to each tiny detail of the story and convinced he had heard it all, Walter ordered Bonnie back into the Thunderbird to tell their guests that the party was over. He was devastated. He could not believe what had happened. His anger cooled to make room for emptiness.

He had lost his mentor. The Bear had been a second father, his protector and best friend. All of that was gone. The most frightening aspect was the future. The Bear represented the opportunity to secure his future. He was striving to achieve a position similar to The Bear's. Ever since his talks with Uncle Archie Walter had been told that the outside world, the so-called legitimate world, was full of people lacking character and integrity. The Mafia represented itself as a tightly knit family where fraternal respect was one of the top priorities. People, so The Bear himself had said, don't lie to you or cheat you in the family. There was a strict code of ethics, wasn't there? Why did The Bear ignore them? His offense was not just against family, it was against a close friend. The rules obviously didn't stand. Fraternal love was a clever way of keeping order. Why had he deluded himself? The Mafia wasn't a family. It was a herd of cattle. Better still, prisoners, all chained together by a common bond of fear, not respect. The whole damn thing fed on fear. The very thing Walter admired and coveted most was The Bear's ability to intimidate. How could he have been such a fool? It was plain to see all along.

Ultimately, he was just a peon in a filthy charade. There was no glamour. No glory either. To make it to the top was a death sentence. The bodies of bosses had been strewn across the country. Some respect! Was this his future, to be like The Bear? To try to seduce a friend's wife? What could he do? No education, no job experience. He was a jewel thief and a smart ass. He obviously wasn't needed either.

"I hate that bastard. I hate them all," he cried out. He was alone again. As he put his hands to his face, one answer came through loud and clear – revenge. That was his future. To kill The Bear would certainly mean the end of the line. Then again, he had nowhere to go anyway.

He looked up. Bonnie was standing off, watching him as he came out of his mumbling trance. "I don't have tomorrow or yesterday or anything else," he spoke. "I have now, right now – The Bear goes down. He's dead."

It was 3:00 A.M. when they arrived home. His father had told him several days earlier about a meeting with The Bear on New Year's morning around 8:30. Walter would be there. He grabbed a .38 snub-nose which he had lifted in a burglary. It was a "throwaway" to be used for a hit and then discarded. Since the gun was stolen, it would be impossible for police to trace it back to Walter. He sat from 3:00 until 5:30 A.M., the gun cradled to his chest, playing the pool game scene in his head over and over. His depression and futility built into anger again, and as the sun began to rise, the anger ignited. He woke Bonnie, dragged her to the car, and headed for his father's office in the Home Bread building in downtown Hollywood. They parked across the street from the building at 6:30. Two hours later a candy-apple-red Eldorado pulled into the parking lot.

The Bear had arrived with three subordinates, goons. Walter waited until the men made their entrance. He went up the elevator and found his father's office door open. It was a holiday, but he made a quick check down the dark hallway. The voices of the men inside the office echoed down the corridor. As he walked into the reception room, his father spotted him.

"Why so early, Walt? What are you doing here?" he asked.

"Why didn't you tell me?" Walter responded.

His father lowered his eyes for a second and then looked at Walter. "I've taken care of it, Walt, there's no problem . . ."

Walter interrupted, "No, you didn't take care of it. You didn't do anything. You figured I wouldn't find out about it and the whole thing would blow over. Well, I found out. And it's a problem."

Walter brushed past his father into the office. The Bear sat with his feet on the desk.

"Hey, kid, how are you doing?" The Bear questioned with a smile.

"Don't 'kid' me," said Walter.

"What's wrong, son?" responded The Bear.

"I just dropped by to ask you about one of Frank Sinatra's old songs. I think it's called 'When and Where', and the chorus goes, 'When are we going out and where will we meet,'" said Walter.

"I don't know what you're talking about." The Bear denied it.

"Do I need to bring Bonnie up to refresh your memory, 'cause she's in the car," Walter shouted.

"Walt, calm down, I just wanted to make sure she was loyal to you. I was looking out for you." The Bear spoke sympathetically.

"Shut up – you're a liar." Walter's voice cracked between the command and the accusation.

-120-

The Bear looked sternly now. "Be careful, Walt. Don't go getting disrespectful – there's a price for it." The Bear was an old hand at confrontation.

Walter was a split second away from a breakdown, his ribs heaving and his hands trembling. Three of The Bear's henchmen moved toward him. In mid-step the snub-nosed .38 special was out and focused on The Bear's stomach, twitching just six inches away. Walter's eyes shot around the room and back at The Bear. The three men stopped. Sweat poured from Walter's body. He was pale, almost dead-looking, a crazed zombie. Deep breaths now turned to gasps, frantic lung-filling gasps to keep up with a heart pumping beyond its means. He had done it. He was holding a gun on the most powerful man he knew.

The Bear sat half a foot and two-thousandths of a second from extinction. He stared at the gun and then back at Walter. He spoke calmly, his voice still tinted with compassion. "You're biting off more than you can chew, kid."

The Bear's ease startled Walter. Was he invincible? Did nothing threaten him? Suddenly the gun grew heavy, like lead, like a fat brick. He was losing. Confused and frustrated, he loosened his grip from the trigger. He felt so tiny, so small and insignificant. Finally he spoke. "I have rights. Laws, family laws. I could kill you right now, or I could walk away with my respect, independent, no longer yours," said Walter.

"Okay, what choice do you want?" The Bear asked, keeping his eyes pinned to Walter's.

"Walk away," Walter whispered.

"What?" asked The Bear.

"Walk away," he shouted back.

"So be it." The Bear lifted his hands. "You are too much; your heart's gonna get you killed one day."

Walter wasn't listening. The gun lay limply in his hand. His mind was sacked with questions for which he had no answers. *What will I do? What have I done? Where? When? What do they think? What am I? And, what have I become?*

Tears welled in his eyes. He wanted someone to hold him, to reach out and give him assurance. There was no one. He had destroyed his relationship with his mother and father, and Bonnie had long ago grown tired of his promises to start a different life. Salerno? What a joke! No friends, no smiles, no laughter. The tears kept rising, and just before they spilled over, Walter forced them back.

The Bear started up in a heavy Italian accent, "This is how we work it. You walk out that door and you're gone — history! I don't know you, I'm not a brother. I'll tell ya, kid, you are the first and last guy to ever pull a gun on me and live. So I call you the 'Crazy Kid.' Now get out of here." He looked at Walter as if to say, "This is the best I can do."

Walter dropped the gun on the desk and walked out. Down the long dark corridor, a numb sensation growing, he walked toward daylight. He was empty and void and tired and lonely and old and confused and oblong and ugly and finished and waiting . . . waiting for truth to emerge, the unpleasant, undeniable truth. Later that night it did.

He had lost a hero to become one. The nickname "Crazy Kid" spread throughout the streets, earning him respect. But that early New Year's morning, as he approached his car, all he knew was that he would never find happiness or peace. He had caught that disease so eloquently described by the Danish philosopher Søren Kierkegaard, "the sickness unto death." There would be new highs and new lows, but with the knowledge that something was missing, the sensation of lacking, he would never be able to really commit himself to anything again. The nickname "Crazy Kid" crowned the end of a part of his life. He had received the title too late. He was neither crazy nor a kid. He was becoming quite serious – seriously dejected and alone.

25

CHAPTER TWENTY-FIVE

Walter continued his work as a Dinnertime Burglar after his split with The Bear. He had always looked on his burglaries as a catapult to a position of power. The Bear had warned him on several occasions that the older he got the harder it would be to jump backyard fences. The Bear's work may have been brutal, but it was not nearly as physically taxing as burglary. The trouble was that Walter no longer wanted to become powerful. Neither the legitimate world nor the Mafia family attracted him. It was not that he had lost his spirit, though his confidence and optimism were clearly sapped; he simply had nowhere to go.

He and Pete Salerno lived in Hollywood, Florida, Walter on Hood Street and Salerno on Johnson Street one block away. They faithfully made their rounds of Miami Shores, Coral Gables, Gables by the Sea, Miami Gardens, Miami Lakes, Jupiter Beach, Hobie Sound, Boca Raton, and Palm Beach. Their earnings were up, but time, which had once proceeded at a hectic and lively pace, seemed to stop. Better pay was not commensurate with better times. The burglaries took on the atmosphere of a graveyard shift at an all-night diner. The carnival-like adventures were over.

Walter eventually found out that Salerno was lying to him about the weekly profits after the fence. He left Salerno – no fuss, screaming, or head banging, he just walked out of Pete's house one night with a calm, "Burn in hell!"

He had more than enough cash saved to live in luxury for the next several years without lifting a finger. It was a perfect time to pacify Bonnie and rebuild a worn relationship, but Walter started exploring new projects, giving Bonnie everything but time and fidelity.

She knew about his affairs. He knew she knew about his affairs. His two children did not know, and it was for their sake that Bonnie remained quiet. No sense in confronting a dead man anyway. She found out about an airline stewardess. Walter respectfully quit seeing her, only to find a substitute. Such was their communication.

The extramarital relationships were unfulfilling – another avenue down. His misery turned to bitterness. He had endless days to do nothing but examine his life. As is often the case, his analyzing procedures were debilitating rather than beneficial. Connecting a long series of half-truths together, he formed one gigantic lie. His discovery was the first thing that had solicited deep emotion in months. He felt alive, not happy, but at least alive. In the darkest confusion and depression one can hate. Walter found hatred an easy and reliable companion. The world deserved his hatred because it had disappointed him. Moreover, he did not need to have a goal to hate. He did not need a plan to hate. He did not even need to select a person to hate. He could hate everyone. He could hate the world collectively, prescind and hate philosophically, or hate specifically. He could hate Bonnie, Salerno, his mother, his father, the grocer, the paper boy, and of course The Bear. He had the time to hate all of them and he did. On March 13, 1973, when Amy Stephenson offered him $25,000 to kill her husband, Walter agreed to hate him too.

26

CHAPTER TWENTY-SIX

Amy Stephenson had made a fortune as the owner of a carpet company given to her by a relative who was a West Coast underboss. As she approached her fiftieth birthday, she married Art Tierra, ten years her junior. Amy was still an attractive woman. She pampered a lovely figure, but Art did not find her beautiful enough. He divorced her and in the process took the carpet company, her jewelry, and a substantial amount of cash. Walter was asked to retrieve her lost fortune and dispose of ungrateful Art.

When Amy met Walter, she expressed some reservations. It was not that she had doubts about liquidating her ex-husband, she relished that thought. She feared that Walter was just another brash young con artist. She explained that several months earlier she had given $5,000 to a man named Tony Moriano to perform the chore. She described him, "about six-two, probably two hundred and sixty pounds, a real monster, and oh yes, he had this long nickel plated gun he showed me."

Walter smiled. "Tony Moriano, did you say?"

"Yes, that was it, Tony Moriano," she responded. Walter

committed to meet her the next day, collect the $25,000 fee, and execute the assignment.

He didn't tell Bonnie about his new job. She didn't ask. The hit was not a major move. He did not grapple with an ethical dilemma. In fact, aside from it's being an excellent opportunity to express his contempt for life, the job promised to be boring. He had faced the prospect of taking life before. Once it was exciting.

The next day, as Donaldson drove him to Amy's house Walter asked the burly man what he had done before he had been hired as his bodyguard and driver.

"Before you and Salerno I ran a congame, you know, a little flimflam here and there," answered Donaldson.

"A little flimflam, John?" Walter laughed.

As they approached Amy's house Donaldson grew noticeably nervous. "Come in with me, John," Walter said sprucely.

No, I think I'll sit this one out, Walt," he responded.

"Come on, John, get out of the car. What's got ya spooked? This is a fifty-year-old lady," Walter jeered.

"No, I'm alright. You know, just a little tired. I'll sit this one out," repeated Donaldson.

"I won't go in without you. I want you to meet this lady. I think you'll find her interesting," said Walter.

The men knocked on the door. Amy called for them to enter. She was shocked. Donaldson looked away pitifully as Walter burst out laughing. "I take it you two have met." He pressed the joke. "Amy, this is John Donaldson, although you probably remember him as Tony Moriano. Tony – I mean John – this is Amy Stephenson."

Amy was not amused and suggested that Walter receive only $20,000 to make up for the $5,000 she had lost to Donaldson. Walter's smile vanished. "Look, lady, whatever you screwed up with John ain't got nothing to do with me. If I don't get twenty-five-thousand you've got no deal and your ex lives," Walter said sternly, suddenly going from laughter to anger.

She hesitated and then asked to speak to Walter privately, pulling him into the bedroom. "Walter, I have an idea," she said, playing with the buttons on his shirt. "Why don't I work some of this bill off?"

Walter walked back into the living room. "Business is business, and I don't mix business with anything else." Her charms were fading, reluctantly she counted out the cash.

Walter tracked down Art Tierra in Tony Roma's Restaurant and Bar on Biscayne Boulevard. The restaurant served an excellent menu, and had become a popular Mafia feeding and drinking hangout. Without a preparatory introduction Walter demanded that Art return the stock and jewelry to Amy Stephenson.

Art Tierra coolly rejected the proposal. He wanted Walter to understand that he was under the protection of the Gallo family. The Gallo family was powerful, but Walter no longer held Mafia families in awe. He had a need, a gnawing hunger to drive things, anything, everything, to an extreme, to push everyone and anyone to the limit. He told Tierra that he was unimpressed with his connections. "I want the stock and jewelry tomorrow, and I want the keys to your Continental now."

Tierra, insulted, flew off waving his arms up and down, screaming about respect and family rights. Walter delivered a sharp backhand to Tierra's face. Blood spurted from his mouth. Walter gave him a final warning. "It's your life. You choose, wise guy, 'cause when I come back, it won't be to hit you in the mouth."

He banged on Amy's door. She had put his life on the line.

That could not be overlooked. She should have known that her ex-husband was "connected." She opened the door, smiling when she recognized Walter. He slapped her across the face with the same force he had used on her ex-husband. The blow knocked four caps from her front teeth. The fifty-year-old woman slumped to the entrance foyer floor, dazed. Before she could collect her dental work, he grabbed her coiffured, tinted hair and dragged her to the bedroom. Donaldson closed the front door to soften her high-pitched, piercing screams. Walter held her face, by her hair, up to a mirror. She opened her mouth to release a steady flow of blood and saliva. The pain was unbearable, and as far as she knew, the ordeal had not ended. She looked into the mirror to catch Walter's eyes. He enjoyed the action. He could kill her, he thought, but he wanted the drama to continue. It enabled him to create more turmoil. He did not want efficiency. He had no destination. He wanted emotional stimulation. The violence was an effective narcotic. It dulled his sensitivity to the utter futility eating away in his guts. He shoved her face close to the mirror, screaming, "Your ex is connected!"

Amy cried out, "I didn't know, Walter, I swear I didn't know, I . . ."

Walter interrupted. "Look at your face, get a good look. Your teeth, you can fix, but plastic surgery won't help you if anything else goes wrong. And my price just went up to $75,000 on top of the $25,000." He shook her head several times before releasing his grip. She collapsed on the tile floor, sobbing.

27

CHAPTER TWENTY-SEVEN

Amy Stephenson worked for an eighty-three-year-old multimillionaire named Martin Stein who lived in New York. She had become his trusted bookkeeper and was placed in a position of considerable authority over his vast holdings. After her grim confrontation with Walter, Amy rushed to New York, had Stein sign four blank checks, and gave them to Walter. She told him that he was welcome to as much as he cared to take.

Walter and Donaldson flew to New York to cash the checks. Initially they were going to make them out for exorbitant sums, but Walter got cold feet. He decided to use the four checks "conservatively." Three checks, totaling $40,000, were cashed in New York. Both men were afraid to cash a final check which had been made out for $20,000. Back in Miami, Donaldson suggested that they open a savings account to legitimize their theft. He opened the account at the Pan American Bank on 163rd Street in North Miami Beach, depositing a $20,000 cashier's check they had gotten from part of the cash. That same morning Donaldson returned and cashed another cashier's check, against the $20,000, for $7,500. Still unsatisfied, Walter went back that afternoon with a check made out for the remainder of the $20,000.

The bank teller told him there would be a short delay. He took a seat in the plush lobby and thumbed a magazine. A few minutes later the vice-president of the bank walked toward him with a security officer. The vice-president asked Walter where the man was who had opened the account that morning. Walter stated that he was unavailable. The security officer informed Walter that he was under arrest and demanded that he empty his pockets. Among other items, Walter pulled out $2,300 cash. The vice-president demanded the remainder of the $7,500 that had been withdrawn earlier. Walter protested, saying the $2,300 was his own money, unconnected to Donaldson's $7,500 withdrawal.

The argument was interrupted by the appearance of Police Detective David Hatterman. Hatterman had been tailing Shaw for months. Shaw, he knew, was a crook, and a boisterous, arrogant one at that, contemptible and blatant. "Looks like you've got your filthy hands caught in the cookie jar, Shaw," taunted Hatterman. "I'm booking you for grand theft."

Walter laughed. "You ain't got nothing on me, Hatterman."

"Didn't you know," responded Hatterman, "there's a millionaire in New York who reported four of his personal checks as stolen? You're busted, Shaw." Hatterman stared into Walter's eyes. Most of the time his job was drudgery, a boring routine. Moments like this made up for it. He spoke with relish. "Let's go check your car."

Donaldson, who had driven Walter to the bank, had disappeared, leaving behind the empty black Mark IV. When Shaw did not return to the car immediately, Donaldson suspected that a problem had developed. Frightened, he stepped out of the car and ran. Sprinting down the highway in a three-piece suit he swore again and again, "I will never listen to Walter Shaw. I will never listen to Walter Shaw."

Hatterman popped open the trunk of the Mark. Walter's two Browning .9 millimeters lay there conspicuously. Hatterman held them up to Walter's face and laughed. "These little jewels registered, Shaw? I'm taking you in scum!"

Walter was booked at the Opalocka police station and was going through routine questioning when a homicide detective named Tom Desivido pulled up a chair and sat down.

"Shaw, what would you say if I said I had a waitress at Big Daddy's bar who says she saw you leave Big Daddy's with Stanley Harris last night?" Desivido asked sarcastically.

"I would say, 'So what'," Walter countered.

"Oh, I guess you haven't heard, have you? Harris was murdered last night. Cut in half by an M-16. We brought him to the morgue in two body bags," Desivido blasted. "Here, look at these." He shoved a set of police photos at Walter. Walter looked at the photographs carefully. Stanley Harris, a good looking guy, six-foot-one, blond and muscular, had been a friend since childhood. The photographs were ghastly. His body had been riddled with bullets and sliced into two distinct pieces. M-16s were not for playing cowboys and Indians. At Big Daddy's, Harris had told Walter that he was in trouble with Ricky Cavarro and requested that Walter join him for what was supposed to be a sit-down. Walter bowed out, saying that he was too tired to accompany him. Actually, Walter wanted nothing to do with Cavarro.

Cavarro, Walter's friend during childhood as well, had built a reputation all his own. He was a feared man. Reputed to be south Florida's premier drug lord, with 150 soldiers, he had declared his independence from the Mafia and lived. His indiscreet murders of DEA agents and rival drug lords prompted mafiosos to steer clear of the wild young maverick.

Walter handed the photographs back to Detective

Desivido, closing his eyes. The photograph could have easily been of a double murder, four pieces, two pieces of Harris's body and two of his own. "Wake up, Shaw," interrupted Desivido. "You'll need to be alert to face a murder rap."

Walter asked for his one telephone call. He dialed his attorney, Paul Pollack. Pollack demanded that Desivido either book Walter on a Murder One charge or stop harassing him. Without solid evidence Desividio reluctantly backed off.

Walter's next appointment was at the Dade County Court House to be arraigned on a grand-theft charge. As he was led down the long corridor he spotted Ricky Cavarro. "Is that how you treat old friends?" Walter asked.

Outside the courtroom Hatterman walked up to Walter with a huge smile. "You're going away for a long time!"

Walter looked back at Hatterman, managing his special arrogant smile, "Hatterman, I'll tell you what, it's eight o'clock. At nine forty-five I'll meet you across the street and buy you some coffee and doughnuts."

Hatterman could not control himself. He burst out, screaming, "You're gone, you sorry lowlife punk, gone – gone, gone, gone!" Walter laughed even harder.

Unfortunately, Hatterman had not learned the full details of the case. Two days earlier, State Prosecutor Nathaniel Barrone had attempted to subpoena Martin Stein. The multimillionaire did not want to trouble himself by flying down to Florida to argue over a paltry $60,000. Moreover, the publicity would be harmful. Stein decided to drop all charges. When the prosecutor approached the bench to inform the judge of Stein's decision, the case was dismissed. Outside the courtroom Hatterman exploded, throwing Shaw's portfolio on the floor and cursing.

"How about the doughnuts and coffee?" Shaw remarked.

Hatterman rushed toward him. "I'm going to make it my

personal business to see that you go to prison for the rest of your life!" he said, shaking his finger in Shaw's face.

"Does this mean you're not hungry?" continued Shaw as he brushed passed him.

Walter had two people to visit after his release. The first was Amy Stephenson, to tell her the deal was off. The second was John Donaldson. He knocked on the door of Donaldson's apartment for a full five minutes. Finally, Donaldson weakly asked who it was.

"It's me, open up," Walter ordered.

As the door opened Shaw broke into laughter. The black-haired giant had bleached his hair into blazing blond and sported a blond moustache. "What in God's name have you done? The heat's off?"

"Now you tell me," Donaldson said dryly.

28

CHAPTER TWENTY-EIGHT

Walter's welcome home from court was not pretty. After celebrating with Donaldson into the early morning, he pulled into his driveway to find that his home had been reduced to a war zone. Police were everywhere.

The house had been sprayed with bullets. His new Mark IV had a bullet hole in the rear quarter panel, and a Cadillac, stolen to use as hit transportation for the Amy Stephenson contract, had been completely destroyed, every window shot out and the body ripped open beyond repair. Several windows in the house had been shot out too. One was in the bedroom occupied by Walter's young daughter. Walter surveyed the damage. The policemen in the driveway walked back to their patrol cars. "Why couldn't you have been in one of those cars, Shaw?" one questioned.

There was no need for an investigation. Walter knew who had committed the act. Several days earlier he had given Pete Salerno's eighteen-year-old nephew, John Morganti, a tip on a gas station ripe for robbing. Shaw told Morganti about the station on the condition that he would receive a ten-percent cut after the station had been "banged out." Morganti did not live up to his promise. Shaw threatened him. The young hood made the mistake of attacking Shaw's house to prove that he was unimpressed by the threat.

It was 2:00 A.M., but settling the account with young Morganti could not be delayed. Walter strapped on two Brownings he had previously tucked away (Hatterman had confiscated the two in Walter's automobile), walked over to Salerno's house, and banged on the door. Walter explained what had happened. "You know, Pete, the terrible thing is, someone is gonna have to die because of this foolishness."

Salerno balked. Walter needed to understand that Johnny Morganti's mother, Salerno's sister-in-law, was connected to Joey P., a powerful New York underboss. Heeding the warning, Walter and Donaldson decided to scare Johnny and retrieve the money. They agreed that, "maybe not Johnny, but one of his buddies is going down." Such disrespect could not go unnoticed. He had not been able to make the hit on Amy's ex-husband. Now, another opportunity had been presented. The goons had shot up his house, one of his kids could have been killed. The meditations on "wasting" one of the vandals pumped extra adrenaline through his body. Adrenaline was killing-juice.

One afternoon a few days later, Walter and Donaldson turned down Hood Street. One of the teenagers who had been with Morganti the night of the shooting came barreling down the street in a Volkswagen. Donaldson veered straight toward him. The teenager left the street to avoid the crash, coming to a rough stop. Walter jumped out of the Continental and held his pistol to the young man's ear. His girlfriend, sitting next to him trembling, began screaming and threatened to get the police. Walter warned the girl to shut up. He motioned for the young man to get out of his car and into the trunk of the Continental.

He refused. Walter spoke calmly. "Either you get in the trunk and take a chance on living or you don't. I'd just as soon kill you right here." Walter's logic was convincing. The Continental sped off, leaving the girlfriend.

They drove to Walter's house to question the young man. Walter struck him in the face repeatedly to loosen jaws that were apparently stuck. Finally he admitted to his participation in the raid. Walter told Donaldson to bring Pete Salerno over. The kid refused to talk again, afraid to rat on Johnny Morganti in front of his uncle. Walter recommenced the assault on his face. "You know, I am so tired of kicking your face in. Talk or I'm gonna kill you. No more baby stuff."

The kid blubbered out the truth. Walter turned to Salerno. "Pete, if that punk nephew of yours repairs my house and my cars, I'll let him live. But I don't care who he's connected to. If he doesn't pay, he's dead."

Two days later Johnny Morganti brought Walter $1,700 and stated that his accomplices did not have money for payment. The next day Walter went to pick up his wife, who was visiting a friend. As Donaldson pulled into the driveway, sixteen-year-old Dale McClain came running out. McClain was Morganti's helpmate. The boy saw Walter and took off running. The big Continental dug in as Donaldson chased the boy down the street. Walter emerged from the window of the car, both Brownings blazing. He fired shot after shot at the youth in broad daylight. For the second time in a week the neighborhood had been turned into a shooting gallery. McClain cut into a large field, and the car buckled as it jumped the curb in pursuit. Walter continued his wild shooting spree until the heavy underbrush became too dense and Donaldson had to stop the car.

Later that afternoon Johnny Morganti showed up, pale-faced and intimidated, to plead for McClain's life. Even though his Uncle Pete warned him that Shaw was bad news, never did he imagine that he was maniac enough to hunt someone down, shoot someone down, in a quiet neighborhood in broad daylight.

Walter agreed to talk to McClain if McClain had the courage to face him. That night the sixteen-year-old made his entrance. He was wearing an expensive gray satin suit, unusual attire for one his age. Underneath he packed a Star .9 millimeter. Before he could open his mouth, Walter slammed him against the wall and took the .9 millimeter. "Are you crazy? Coming to my house packing a gun?" asked Shaw.

"A man's got to carry a weapon," McClain responded weakly.

Walter and Donaldson laughed. "You want to live, punk?"

"Yeah," uttered McClain sheepishly.

"You've got guts, I'll say that. You want to work for me and live well?" Shaw asked.

McClain was awestruck by the unexpected offer. Could this be his reward for destroying a house and two cars? By the end of the evening Shaw had hired not only McClain, but McClain's uncle, Marshall Perlow, and his friend Gene Tyce. Tyce was nineteen and Perlow twenty-one. Walter's hot-and-cold temperament never ceased to astonish Donaldson – one minute a killer, the next a kingpin. Walter casually dismissed his intentions to take McClain's life. He was never bothered by a need for consistency or determination. Everything came straight from the hip.

McClain, along with a covey of local youth, viewed Shaw as a hero – a genuine gangster, a gun-toting and shooting mobster with fancy cars and a chauffeur. Walter had been feared, hated, admired, cursed, threatened, and loved. He had never been worshipped. The elevation given him by these young associates boosted his ego, bloated it, and with them he could practice his talents at manipulation unhindered. He had reached the status of undisputed boss, at least in an area of a few blocks. Perlow, Tyce, and McClain didn't seem to mind his cruelty as long as it kept them supplied with spending money.

Perlow had been dating a lovely girl, who was wealthy, attractive, and overbearing. When Perlow brought her to meet Shaw, she began questioning him and making various demands. Walter ignored her. She continued smarting off. Never one to share authority, especially around his young associates, Walter stormed at her, "Either you shut up or I'll put you in the damn oven."

Perlow lost his girlfriend, but kept his new job. Weeks later he had a more direct taste of Walter's wrath. Perlow, an avid marijuana smoker, developed the ugly habit of smoking joints to brace himself before scores. One night he had been positioned under the roof of a house to help break Walter's fall when he jumped with the loot. It wasn't a dangerous mission. Walter planned to sit on the edge of the roof and slide off. Perlow's job was to break his fall and keep everything quiet and safe. When Walter made his move, Perlow stood immobile, dumbfoundedly watching him crash to the ground. He was simply "out of his head," floating, and forgot his assignment. Once safely back home, Shaw dragged him into the house by his ear.

"What the hell's the matter with you?" Walter blasted.

"I smoked a little," Perlow admitted, embarrassed.

"Ah, you smoked a little. You idiot, I told you never to smoke, pop pills, shoot needles, or do anything else before we go out. You get high and I nearly break my legs." Walter paced in front of Perlow. Then he bent down, pulled off his shoe, and struck Perlow in the face with it. Bonnie ran in as he delivered his third blow.

"Now what?" he asked her.

"Stop it," she cried.

"Okay, I'll stop. You want me to stop hitting this dumb idiot. I say I'll stop." He rushed into the kitchen and returned with a carving knife and a fork.

"What's going on, Walt?" Perlow protested weakly. He did not wait for the answer. Walter lunged at him and Perlow, sobering by the half-second, ran for his life, with Walter flashing and waving the carving knife and fork right behind him. Bonnie charged after both of them. It was too late. Walter had cornered Perlow. He stuck the carving knife and long fork in Perlow's face.

"If you ever smoke dope again before a job, I'll pluck your damn eye out and eat it!" Walter said, thereby initiating one of the most effective and immediate narcotic rehabilitation programs in history. Perlow decided that Shaw's crude surgical skills and instruments, combined with a lack of local or general anesthesia, would result in great duress. He opted, there and then, not to have his eye carved out, not to smoke marijuana, and not to cross Walter, ever.

Shaw used similar tactics on Tyce and McClain. He would wave his pistol around to capture an attentive audience and then point the pistol to obtain a loyal subject. Once the novelty of having a gang of ardent admirers wore off, Shaw's cruelty became more intense. The boys submitted to Walter's control for a more significant reason than hero worship, however. Walter was a master. He had graduated, the third edition of the great cat burglars. First Davis, government-trained and lethal, then Salerno, street-tough and gutsy, and finally Walter, intense and fearless. The third generation superseded the predecessors. He was sure of this. Night after night his raids netted thousands of tax-free dollars. No credit or collection problems and no deposits or records. And no house was safe. Walter knew where to go, how to go, when to go, how long to stay, and what to take.

The gang did hundreds of homes without a single close incident, without one arrest. Walter had that touch. After the first five or six houses the young hoods were sure their luck was running out. Five more and they were convinced that there would never be a day of reckoning.

29

CHAPTER TWENTY-NINE

At last Walter had gained what he had craved since meeting Archie Geanunzio at the age of ten – power. Salerno, once his mentor and teacher, then his competitor, was, after the Howard Johnson's sit-down, his allegiant follower. When Salerno extracted himself from an indictment in 1974, he returned to Shaw and worked with him on his terms. Walter had his own gang of Dinnertime Burglars, and he commanded and received widespread respect on the streets. His lifelong pursuit had come into focus and neared fruition. Instead of contentment, he found misery. After paying such an enormous price for success, it seemed so meaningless. Bonnie continued to watch their marriage drift apart, and Walter, finding novel ways to be despicable, no longer spent time with his children. He had always been a good father, but now he even loathed the responsibility his children presented.

Nothing was sacred and no one stood above his cruelty. On Christmas Eve of 1974, he told Bonnie he was going out to get a hamburger, promising, "I'll be back in ten minutes to play Santa."

He forgot both his promise and his hunger and drove to a bar to spend the evening sharing Christmas "spirits" with a female companion. Bonnie sat in the living room waiting for him through the night. He stumbled through the door, still drunk, at five o'clock on Christmas morning. Bonnie cried, "That must have been some hamburger."

His new gang was afforded similar inconsiderate treatment. In a *Miami Herald* feature article on burglar-turned-informant Gene Tyce, entitled "A Teen's Journey into the Underworld," writer Robert Liss reported that the nineteen-year-old Tyce said of Shaw, "He ruled with guns and threats." Liss continued, "Shaw had to be forceful to keep his cohorts in line. He sometimes carried a gun for that purpose."

Walter created tension by bilking the young burglars out of their share. He cheated because he hated, not because he needed the money. The more intensely his young associates reacted to his financial sabotage, the more enjoyable for him. Ironically, at each level of intimidation, with each added ordeal, Tyce, along with the others, admired him more. Walter was a hero. The youths were confused, but they remained loyal admirers. Shaw's blatant brutality, in fact, led them to respect him. Violence was what they expected from a crime hero, and the greater the violence, the greater the stature.

Shortly before Christmas of 1974, Gold Coast Steel Construction Company, which Walter had acquired through extortion, laid off a large percentage of its laborers. One man's wife had just given birth to a baby boy and the worker desperately needed economic assistance. The young father, Bill Marlow, visited Walter, pleading for a job. "Anything to make it," he said.

Walter agreed to take him out for just one night to solve his economic woes. To see him through until the night arrived, Walter advanced him a few dollars.

On the 15th of January, Marlow got his opportunity. Walter assigned him to Dale McClain and Gene Tyce. Scheduled to see Pete Salerno later that night, Walter delivered instructions to the three. "The job is easy, Tyce will drive to Tamarac and I've already shown Dale a good house there. Strictly kid's stuff. Pete and I will be here when you return. You won't have any problems."

There were problems, big ones, and these years later, when Walter relates the gruesome events which unfolded that fateful night, he grips the table edge or chair arm, his eyes dart rapidly as if trying to focus, and then spillover. For six weeks running the police had been staking out the neighborhood waiting for Shaw's return as he made his circuit. Walter had selected a Spanish-style two-story home, working on a reliable tip that the lady of the house owned several hundred thousand dollars' worth of jewelry. When McClain and Marlow arrived, they confronted an unusual challenge. The homeowners had already gone upstairs to watch television. The master bedroom was upstairs as well. Dale turned to Marlow. "Sorry, it's no go."

Bill Marlow looked at the young thief, "Please, Dale, my kid, man, let's just do one for my kid."

Marlow, desperate to provide for his wife and baby, and seeing the provision evaporating, pleaded with Dale not to abort the mission, and Dale, against everything that Walter had taught, yielded. They positioned themselves around a back window for entry. As Dale reached for the window, he spotted a large white object out of the corner of his eyes. He stood still. Slowly he focused on the blurred image that waited in the darkness. It was a white golf cart. He grabbed Marlow by the collar of his shirt and turned to make a break. The golf cart's lights flashed on. A voice shouted "Freeze."

They ran. Dale, who had been under pressure before, kept his sense of direction and headed straight toward a lake, a hundred yards away. Marlow, frantic, ran one way and then another, finally choosing a dead end; he was trapped by a high fence. Like a wounded animal he screamed out, banged against the fence as if trying to go through it, and then turned to run for the lake.

When he was halfway to his destination the cops spotted him and yelled "Freeze" again. This time he froze, shaking and crying, and probably wishing with all his soul that he had signed up for welfare after losing his job instead of attempting a break-in. As he raised his hands in submission a cannon blast rocked the peaceful neighborhood and echoed into the still night air. The deadly .357 magnum found its target, and Marlow, who had been standing obediently, hands over head, knelt on the ground watching his intestines pour from his midsection. "God, God, God, God help me," he screamed out, then, adrenaline pumping madly to save an already fatally wounded body, he lifted himself up and ran toward the lake. A second hollow crack violated the nighttime calm. A pump shotgun this time. He lay dead.

The two policemen rushed to the riddled body as it convulsed and oozed blood. One of them pulled out a .45. A final, unneeded explosion reverberated through Tamarac, Florida. The bullet pierced Marlow's right temple, ripped through his skull, shredding his brain, and passed out the opposite side of his head. The policemen turned and yelled toward the lake, ordering Dale out of the water. The men chuckled as they cuffed Dale. Dale looked only once at Marlow's head. It had literally exploded. The image raped his mind, destroying all innocence. He welled up with tears, indignant that the police would commit such a crime, forgetting that he was a burglar. One of the officers could not resist, "Well, I guess Walter Shaw's glory days are over."

"What do you mean?" Dale stated defiantly. "That ain't

Walter Shaw."

The officer bent down and eased what was left of the bloody mask off the mutilated head. Facial features had merged into hamburger meat, but enough could be identified to determine that the man was clearly not Shaw. "Damn it!" the detective cursed.

They had monitored the neighborhood for six weeks for a specific target. Not for burglars in general, but for Shaw in particular. He had eluded trap after trap. There were many close calls, but the good guys always came short. When they watched his house, he taunted them. He would drive by a tail car smiling and waving. He owned a Rolls-Royce outright, lived in a several-hundred-thousand-dollar house and had recently put a down payment on a powder-blue Ferrari. He was loud mouthed, humiliating. After years of cat and mouse the police had failed at every turn in the maze. Shaw made fools out of them. So, Walter believes, on that cold January night the officers had decided – though they never spoke it out loud and perhaps it only lurked in their subconscious – that trying to end his career in the courtroom was too risky.

A judge could be duped, a jury misled. They knew Shaw was guilty. They could serve immediate, final justice. They did not want incarceration, they wanted a casket. At last, they thought, Shaw was finished. It had turned into a gruesome blunder. They were embarrassed. They missed again. This time, however, a young husband, attempting a criminal act for the first time, lay on the ground, dead. He too was a loser, but for him the stakes had been much higher.

He never saw his young wife or newborn son again. He decided to enter crime on a one-shot gamble to support his family. One burglary, that was all he wanted. Soon, he had been assured, his old job would be available again. He did not like Walter's life-style. He felt comfortable working by the sweat of his brow. He called it earning a living, his wife said. Stealing a living was cowardice. But with his back against the wall, he vowed to his wife, "Just this once, honey, for you and the baby."

The squad cars moved in to arrest Gene Tyce, who was waiting several blocks down the street. The seventeen-and-nineteen-year-old thugs, McClain and Tyce, were hauled to jail, separated, and subjected to an intimidating interrogation procedure which culminated in warnings to both: If they did not cooperate and provide information on Shaw, they would face a murder rap. "What murder? I didn't murder anybody," each protested in turn.

The detectives embellished a strange twist in Florida law. A death that occurred in the commission of a crime was automatically the responsibility of the accomplices. The crude ploy was fifty-percent effective. Dale McClain looked at the interrogating officer and proclaimed, "Book me, I'll never say nothing against Walt."

Gene Tyce, in another room and frightened beyond loyalty, uttered, "What do you need?"

Dale McClain was hauled to a juvenile detention center. At 12:00 P.M. he placed his one allowed telephone call.

"Walt, Bill's dead. Get everything out of your house. I think Gene's talking." Click, the line was dead. Walter was sitting on the couch with Bonnie. Across from them sat Salerno and Linda Marlow's uncle. Walter stared at Pete.

"What's wrong, Walt?" asked Salerno.

"Are you Okay?" seconded Bonnie.

His eyes turned toward the ceiling and he replied softly, hardly a whisper. "Bill's dead, cops killed him."

Linda's uncle rose from his chair. "We've got to tell her before the police do," he said somberly.

"I will, the whole damn thing is my fault," Walter said.

Bonnie cried steadily the entire trip to Bill Marlow's house.

Walter did not look at her. He knew what she was thinking. He was thinking the same thing. The bullets that had killed Bill Marlow were intended for him. He tried to prepare consoling words for Bill's wife. They did not come. He wanted to feel sadness, grief, but he felt numb and emotionless. He deserved the shooting, not Marlow. He had sown the bitter seeds and he should have reaped the deadly harvest. For weeks he had been dejected, even up to the point of wanting to die. Now he realized, any life is a good life, and whether miserable or glorious, it is worth fighting to keep. That was the second countercomponent that greased the wheels of the Mafia and made it run. Regardless of how empty life became for a Mafia soldier or boss, the alternative to it was unacceptable. The Mafia was able to run on fear because the will to survive ran so strong. The Bear, who hardly had what outsiders would call a life, fought to live. Tom Palmer fought to live. Salerno fought to live. Sacco fought to live. Not to live well, just to stay alive. It came down to that. Walter had been pursuing the wrong dream. Now, with this prophetic police slaughter, he understood that in the syndicate it's not the aspiration to glory or power that energizes. It is the drive to remain alive. That, more than anything else, separated Walter's world from all others.

Walter half-closed his eyes and made a promise to himself, almost a prayer. He would fight. A riveting wave of emotions pushed through his body. He had a goal. He dreamed of survival in an increasingly dangerous world.

30

CHAPTER THIRTY

Walter knocked on the door, and Linda rushed to open it. As her four guests walked inside, she pointed to a table loaded down with sandwiches, chips, and beer. "To celebrate Bill's first and last burglary," she laughed. There was silence. "What's wrong, did Bill get arrested?" she asked.

"No," Walter said.

"Oh, well thank God, for a minute there you had me scared."

"Linda . . . Bill is dead," Walter said softly.

He reached for her, but she ran across the room, screaming and throwing the sandwiches and beer. Her uncle dodged his way to her, grabbed her, and pinned her against the wall. She spit and screamed to free herself until she was exhausted. She looked at Bonnie. "My baby, my baby boy. I gave him a baby boy. Ah please . . . God . . . damn them, damn them . . ."

Walter could not take any more. He and Salerno walked outside. Several minutes later the police arrived.

"Sorry, Walt, is she in there?" asked an officer.

"Oh, that's real funny. Are you sorry you killed a two-month old's father, or are you sorry you didn't kill me?" he shot back.

"I wasn't there, Walt. The guy must have pulled a gun or something," the officer responded.

"Bullshit, he didn't carry a gun. I don't allow that and you know it. Pete never carried a gun, I never carried a gun, but since you guys are butchers, I can guarantee I'll be carrying a gun the next time. Remember that, 'cause on the next bust it will be the other way around. A dead cop – do you hear me? . . . A stinking dead cop."

Bonnie went with Linda to the morgue to identify the body. When she came back she told Walter that if he ever went out again, she would leave him. "That was supposed to be you," she cried. "I love you Walt, please stop. Just come back home." He made the appropriate promises and called his lawyer.

Tom Cazell finally awoke to answer the phone. Walter quickly related the night's events. Cazell, according to Walter, then called the mayor of Oakland Park near Fort Lauderdale. The mayor, Walter had reason to believe, was Mafia-backed and loyal. At 5:00 A.M., the mayor located Tyce who had been hidden by police. Tom Cazell arranged to see him. He promised to pay his bond and pledged that Walter would let him live if he would shut up. Tyce was adamant. He did not want bond. He was safer in jail, he believed. Walter couldn't get to him there. Next Cazell bailed out Dale McClain.

Later that morning the mayor learned that Tyce was ratting on Salerno as well as Walter. He was even disclosing information about a reliable Florida Dinnertime fence. Tyce had pertinent information. Walter prepared himself for trouble.

A week later John Donaldson and Walter were driving down I-95 when they noticed that all the exits were blocked. Five or six squad cars surrounded Walter's black Continental, forcing it off the road. A dozen or more officers disembarked from the squad cars, their shotguns clicking, ready to go.

A *Hollywood Sun-Tattler* article about Shaw by staff writer Jim Whiteshield detailed the arrest from the perspective of Detective Sergeant Marco Cerintelli. Shaw, he stated, had to be "removed forcibly" from the car. "He didn't say much. He's a real pro." Tyce had squealed and Shaw was booked, his second major arrest.

31

CHAPTER THIRTY-ONE

Several months prior to the Marlow killing Walter's first arrest had occurred as a result of his last working partnership with Pete Salerno. Thirty-three-year-old Ralph Grandinett told Salerno that he had some racket friends from Chicago who needed a hefty cocaine purchase. Walter contacted a close friend, a drug dealer, who provided coke to an elite clientele. He boasted that several Dolphin football players were among them. The men from Chicago were supposed to bring a down payment of $300,000. Neither Salerno nor Walter wanted to get involved in the drug-trafficking business, but the $300,000 was persuasive. Walter decided on a plan of action. He and Salerno would get a sample of cocaine from Walter's friend, present it to the Chicago men, accept the $300,000, cuff the men, and depending on their reaction, either ship them back to Chicago or permanently silence them. Grandinett was to meet the men at the airport and take them to his house on Southwest 33rd Street in Miramar.

Walter packed his two Browning .9 millimeters. Salerno carried a Colt Python .357 magnum. Salerno was not pleased with Shaw's contingency plan of "permanent silence" in the event of trouble, but eatenup with litigation costs related to an indictment in 1974, he decided to go along. The $300,000 seemed like such an easy grab. They arrived at Grandinett's house around midnight. The two Chicago racketeers smiled and tried to be friendly. Walter interrupted the chatter. "Let's deal now."

Salerno grew edgy. He was trained for details. One of the men wore cowboy boots. "You boys from Chicago, huh?" he began.

Walter interrupted him, "Pass the attachés."

"We want to test the stuff," one of the men said.

Walter threw the plastic bags across the room. One of the men slid the briefcase toward him. The two men were seated on the couch. Walter and Salerno stood opposite them. Grandinett sat in an easy chair near his friends.

"86.7 percent," called out one of the men, pleased, and then, turning to Grandinett, he asked to see the counterfeit money.

"What's going on?" asked Walter.

"What's going on? What's it to you? My friends are going to buy some of my famous funny money." Grandinett shot back. Walter grunted. The men flipped through the money.

"Aren't you going to open the case?" one asked Walter. Walter patted the side of the attaché without taking his eyes off the man who had just spoken.

"It better be here," he said. Walter opened the case; it wasn't the full $300,000 but it was enough. Besides, it was much too late to back out. He closed it and nodded to Salerno. Salerno whipped out the big magnum and Walter cocked one of his Brownings.

"Freeze, guys, it's over," Walter said sarcastically. Grandinett began protesting, "What in the hell are you trying to pull here? We had a deal."

"Shut up, Ralph, you're getting on my nerves," Walter responded. Grandinett sunk back into his easy chair, dumbfounded. "Wrong," blasted Walter. "On the floor, all three of you, on the floor, face down." Grandinett started to say something but was interrupted by the point of Walter's pistol.

One of the men, lying face down, spoke. "Hey, Shaw, can I get something out of my pocket?"

Walter froze. Grandinett, and most everyone these days, knew Walter by his alias, "Archie Peter Lewis." Grandinett did not know Walter's real name. The man on the floor should not have known it either. He began to lose his concentration. His first reaction was to kill the man but what if he were a . . . no, he couldn't be. "Go ahead, but if you come out with anything besides a handkerchief, I'm blowing your damn head off," Walter said.

The prostrate man pulled out his wallet and handed it to Walter. Walter looked through it, then burst into laughter. He turned to Grandinett. "You've known these guys since they were kids?" He doubled over, laughing. Grandinett, confused and frightened, nodded his head. Walter's mood flipflopped. He screamed, "You're a liar! You just met these guys. No Chicago. No nothing. You're just a greedy bastard. Look at this ID. It says BROWARD COUNTY SHERIFF'S OFFICE, YOU IDIOT!"

Salerno slumped to the carpet.

Detective Bowers, comfortable on the floor, explained that the house was surrounded. "You walk out of here without me and you're wasted, Shaw."

Walter and Salerno dropped their guns without prodding, and exchanged places with the Chicago mobsters turned sheriff's deputies.

As they were cuffed Walter began laughing again,

throwing one wisecrack on top of another. "I'll be out in a few hours, hope it was worth it to you, Sergeant Bowers. All this work for a few hours, lock-up time."

Bowers turned to him in the squad car, warning him to keep quiet. Walter grew more abrasive. Bowers exploded, "Shaw, either shut up or I'll pistol-whip you across the mouth. One more thing, wise guy, we've got you in a ringer. This ain't no burglary charge. This is possession, distribution, and sale of cocaine."

"Wait a minute, you know we were here to bust out some cash, what do you mean possession, distribution, and sale?" Walter asked, fearful now.

"I mean you're finally going to jail, Shaw," Bowers answered confidently, "for a long time."

32

CHAPTER THIRTY-TWO

Just as a chicken, head severed from its body, continues to wildly thrash for life though there is no hope for it, so Walter continued to believe his arrests were minor setbacks, when infact they were death knells. Transported to the Hollywood, Florida jail after the blockade episode on I-95, and charged with breaking and entering, he posted a $6,500 bond, secure in the knowledge that a jury would never accept the testimony of a nineteen-year-old over his own. Weeks earlier Walter had been arrested on a state charge of conspiracy to distribute cocaine, in the case of mistaken identity.

Walter was arrested less than a month later on another breaking-and-entering charge. Gene Tyce had dozens of juicy burglaries to describe in graphic detail. The police examined his testimony, gleaned from it those burglaries that would likely result in a conviction, and arrested Walter for them, one at a time. Each single arrest brought a new indictment and required a new bond, and a new defense. Still optimistic, Walter confidently posted the bonds. Bondsmen were mopping up. Then, several months later, he was arrested on a federal charge of counterfeiting. The arrest-postbond-arrest chain of events mercilessly lasted through six months and six arrests. The final of the series was on a federal charge of conspiracy to distribute cocaine. Walter sat in a Fort Lauderdale jail cell after this arrest, dejected. With his financial resources drained, he was forced to borrow bond money from a friend of The Bear. Eddie Perrone, himself a bondsman, put up the bail. Walter had sold his house to pay bonds and mounting attorney fees. His new home was Miami Beach's Tangiers Hotel on Collins Avenue.

The days were laborious. Bonnie tried to keep his two children quiet, reminding them to give their father peace and time to think. The hotel space was cramped. Every so often his young son or daughter would demand to know why they had to live in a hotel. Walter never answered. He stared blankly and then left the hotel to go for long walks. His children's innocent questions were penetrating. Why? Really, why? The magnitude of his dilemma crashed down.

The cards were stacked against him. If he won all six cases, things would be like they used to be. But to lose even one case meant the unthinkable – hard time. Prison was a concept so revolting that he could not seriously face it. His usually vivid imagination refused to picture himself behind bars, refused to even acknowledge it as a possibility. No one, even the most hardened, could prepare for incarceration. Walter could not even try. Somehow he would extricate himself. He always landed on his feet. He told family and friends as much, even though he was sinking low and heavy at the thought of standing trial. His mental activity was high, but he had little to do other than either walk or peer at some silly program on television.

Weeks dragged by. He had not earned a single dollar. Eddie Perrone visited to be reimbursed for the bond money. When Walter told him he was broke, Perrone started leaning on him.

Late one night three men burst into Walter's room waving revolvers. John Donaldson lumbered out of the bathroom with his nickel-plated Browning .9 millimeter cocked, ready to spill blood. Walter, who had been aimlessly strolling the beach, walked into the middle of the showdown. He pushed past the three men and told Donaldson to put his weapon away. "I don't want no bloodshed in front of my kids," he explained.

Donaldson let out a frustrated sigh as Bonnie gathered her two children. "But Walt...," Donaldson began, still holding his position.

"No!" Walter shouted. "Not in front of my babies." Donaldson twitched uneasily amid the cries of two frightened children. Bonnie was silent, resolutely attempting to shield her children from the world, covering their tear-filled eyes. They were all she had left. She had lost Walter, a long time ago. Soon, though she tried not to think about it, she would lose him forever.

"No, John," Walter commanded again.

Finally Donaldson put his Browning back into its holster and one of the men jabbed a pistol barrel into Walter's ribs. "That was smart, Shaw, now just keep up the good thinking," the thug said. Walter was escorted out of the room. From the balcony of the hotel he saw a black Continental and Eddie Perrone – his destination.

Perrone, standing at the rear of the vehicle, ordered Walter into the trunk. "You can say no and die here or get in and take your chances," said Perrone bluntly.

Walter shrank back. Just months before, he had the money, he did the lending, he held the gun, he gave the orders, and he forced others into the trunk of his Continental. This brutal reversal dug into his guts. His world hung upside down.

The transition was sudden, leaving him no time to prepare or escape. Now it was he who had no home or car, it was he who had no money and had to borrow, and it was he who followed orders - ironically, orders to get into the trunk of a Continental.

Walter looked up at Bonnie and his two children who were watching from the window of the hotel room. He waved, whispered a solemn "I love you," and crawled into the trunk, degraded and alone, bent and hunched over, pitiable, like a mangy dog. Bonnie huddled the children close to her, their heads pressed tight against her hips. She hated Walter for what he had done to her and the family, but she had never wanted to see him lowered to the level of a subservient lackey. In spite of all his inconsideration, she did not want him broken.

Around 3:00 A.M. Perrone stopped for breakfast. He let Walter out of the trunk. Walter asked if he could make a quick telephone call. "Why not," Perrone answered thoughtlessly.

The Bear was under investigation by the F.B.I. and his phone had been subjected to taps for weeks. Walter calmly dialed The Bear's number. Before Perrone could stop him he blurted out, "This creep Perrone is taking me to Lauderdale in the trunk of his car."

Perrone jerked the phone from his ear. "You think you're clever, don't you?" he said.

"I think I saved my life. The FBI and every police department in south Florida will know where I am and who I'm with." Walter answered.

"Let me tell you something, wise guy," Perrone shot back. "If I decide to waste you, nobody can stop me."

Perrone, about five-eleven, grew up in Brooklyn, receiving his education from the streets. He had black hair, which covered the back and sides of his head. The front of his head was bald, accentuating his brown eyes and pockmarked skin. He was an ugly, uncultured sort, who aside from his bonding business did a considerable trade in drugs, pimping, and pornography. Walter had taken a huge gamble by calling The

Bear. For the time being the filibuster was successful. Perrone angrily commanded him to reenter the trunk.

Later that morning Bonnie showed up at Perrone's office in Fort Lauderdale with Mike Grudiadoria. Bonnie had called Grudiadoria, one of Walters friends, to get help. Mike and Bonnie walked into the office with an attaché case. Mike placed the case on Walter's lap and took a seat behind him. Walter sat across the desk from Perrone. Grudiadoria tapped the chair repeatedly, trying to tip Walter. Inside the attaché case Bonnie had placed several thousand dollars' worth of her last pieces of jewelry. Grudiadoria too had added a contribution, which nestled inside the attaché. The long-barreled .38 revolver was a striking contrast to Bonnie's jewelry. Walter popped open the case.

Perrone could not see the contents of the case, but a knowing smile came to his face. "Listen, we can do this hard, or we can do this easy. I would be willing to bet that you have a gun in there. Let me tell you now that you don't want a shoot-out because you won't get out of this office alive," Perrone said.

Walter smiled back. "All I've got is some jewelry."

"You know I don't want jewelry, but because we have mutual friends, and because you grew up in the neighborhood, I'll give you thirty days. I'll hold the jewels for thirty days to give you another chance to come up with the cash."

Walter accepted Perrone's terms and stood to leave. As he walked from the office Perrone called out, "Shaw, tell me, was there a gun in that case?"

Walter turned back. "You'll never know."

The trip back to Miami was quiet. Walter tried to digest the parameters of his situation. Both the legitimate world and his old world held imminent danger. Aside from the six court cases, he had to raise money to pay Perrone. The kidnapping was beneficial. It had shaken off his lethargy. He was broke. He

-161-

had to have money. Collecting shells along the beach and sucking on self-pity would not provide lawyers for the legal battles ahead. It was time to go to work.

He contacted Salerno. The old pro needed money too. Together they banged out enough money through burglary, to satisfy Perrone and Walter's lawyers. After being paid, Perrone called Walter to tell him that he had located Gene Tyce; this was his way of demonstrating to Walter that he harbored no ill feelings. "They're keeping him at the Miami Lakes Fire Department. Just say the word and I'll take care of him."

"No," Walter assured him, "I can beat it in court, leave the kid alone." But the night before his first court date Walter's outlook changed. Donaldson visited him. Shaw, for one of the few times in his life, let down his guard. There was little need for pretense. The old friends talked man to man. "John, I think I'm going away . . ."

"No, Walt, don't say that," Donaldson interrupted.

"Just listen," Shaw continued, "Please take care of my wife and kids." Donaldson pledged his support and left at Shaw's request. There was nothing more to discuss. Donaldson was worried. His boss had lost his way. Shaw's eyes sunk back into their sockets, bloodshot and blackened from lack of sleep. He looked like a rabid animal. He had lost weight and his mental stability was going too. Unshaven and dazed, it was the best Walter would look for a long time.

33

CHAPTER THIRTY-THREE

As Shaw trudged reluctantly toward the courtroom, his lawyer, Matt Cockman, assured him that Eugene Tyce would not stand as a credible witness. Moments before court was scheduled to open, he and Cockman were called into the judge's private chamber. State's attorney Donnie Williams explained that the state was prepared to reduce Shaw's sentence to two years if he would plead guilty. Judge Louis Wiessing as Walter remembers it, joined in, adding that if Shaw was found guilty by the jury, Wiessing himself would pull Shaw's bond and smear his name throughout the media, which, of course, would not help him with other charges and trials pending. Walter spurned the trade-off. He, along with Cockman, was confident that Tyce would be foiled on the witness stand. What jury would believe a nineteen-year-old who himself had been arrested for breaking and entering? And what about the murder? Couldn't Tyce be held partially responsible for that? Wasn't Tyce trying to save himself by lying about Shaw? These were the questions Cockman would force the jury to think long and hard about. And Tyce, Walter knew, melted under pressure. If Tyce could be discredited as a reliable witness, then Shaw would go free. The state's case hinged on Tyce's accounts.

Nevertheless, in spite of the logic about Tyce, Walter was queasy as he left Judge Wiessing's chambers. He had committed to face a jury. There was no turning back. He consoled himself with the knowledge that he had made his choice. He would fight. Anyhow, two years behind bars was not a bargain for a man who had been free all of his life. He walked to a pay phone and called Bonnie. She promised to be in court. At twelve noon she arrived with the two children to watch jewel thief, hit man, extortionist, con man, husband, and father, Walter Thiel Shaw, Jr., face a first-degree charge of breaking and entering.

The trial should have been fairly routine. It was not. The courtroom was charged with energy. Walter had sensed it the night before when he had asked Donaldson to safeguard his wife and children "just in case." His past was closing in. His habitual taunting directed at law enforcement officers suddenly became his humiliation. In the past, whenever he had a run-in with the law, he coyly told officers, "Nothing personal, guys, it's just a business." He had laughed at the bungling detectives for years.

When he walked into the courtroom, he saw the forty-man task force that had been tracking him for six months. They were smiling. He looked again. Odd, they were all wearing T-shirts, the same T-shirts. He looked more closely. What he saw lifted him out of his nervous stupor, made him both proud and angry, pushed him into an arena, and forced him to become the grand actor again. He lost control. He began to blaze; laughing, confident, completely incoherent. On each T-shirt was a silk-screen of his face and a caption which read: "NOTHING PERSONAL GUYS, IT'S JUST A BUSINESS."

His ego bleated out a cry of gratification. He was important, certainly not in a positive way, but nevertheless important. Who but an important man, could draw such a crowd. T-shirts! They wore T-shirts bearing his likeness and his eloquent quotation. He began to buzz as if intoxicated. Why not spin a few yarns on the witness stand and tell them how "bad" I really am?

His mind fought his ego. This was not a circus, it was a trial. *Damn it*, I've got to wake up.

Crack.

Judge Wiessing pounded his gavel to call the court to order. Walter looked up realizing whether he played or prayed, it did not matter. His fate and his life were not in his own hands – *strange feeling.* One of life's greatest treasures is freedom, and his freedom, whether he would have it or not, would be determined by other people. He had no control or say in the matter. He was helpless. He felt like a child, only the proceedings did not concern childish things, they concerned his liberty.

The trial pressed on. The prosecutor hammered mercilessly at the defense presented by Walter's attorney. Cockman did not seem serious enough. He was weak, too nice. There was no doubt where Judge Wiessing stood, Walter thought. *The guy is hungry. He's just waiting to bury me. It's my life, man. The jury is vacillating. One minute for me, the next against me.* He wanted to take the stand, explain everything, use his charm and persuasion. He could sway people, but Cockman advised him to keep quiet. Suddenly, before he could catch up with what was taking place, *Crack!* ... The gavel came down again.

It was over.

The trial had taken nearly ten hours. The jury returned with its verdict. Walter turned and cast a glazed stare at Bonnie. The ten-hour proceedings seemed to him like minutes. His throat contracted and his pulse quickened as the judge read the jury's decision. This circus, which featured him yet never allowed him to perform, was over. On June the 15, 1975, at 10:28 P.M., Walter Thiel Shaw, Jr., was found guilty as charged.

His heart jerked deep inside though he did not jump up or scream. He heard Bonnie take a deep sigh in preparation for a river of tears. He looked back for her, his only source for help. Instead he saw forty T-shirts which read: "NOTHING PERSONAL GUYS, IT'S JUST A BUSINESS." His face, plastered across the stomachs of forty happy men, stared back at him, a broken-mirror effect. This was their day. They stood to salute him irreverently. When the bailiff cuffed him, he asked for a small favor. "Bathroom, I need to use the bathroom."

Gene Tyce, in the restroom already, jumped back nervously when Walter was led in. Walter ignored him and walked slowly to a urinal. He had come in to vomit. He needed to vomit, had to vomit, but he couldn't in front of Tyce. "Why didn't you kill me?" whispered Tyce.

"Because you're nineteen," Shaw answered.

34

CHAPTER THIRTY-FOUR

Twenty-one-year-old Marshall Perlow, who stood trial with Walter, was headed for jail too. "Don't worry, I'll have us out of here before noon tomorrow," Walter promised. Bonnie sold his Cadillac to get the money for the appeal bond. Judge Wiessing denied bond, and Walter and Marshall were placed in a ten-man cell. The eight other men with whom they shared their new home were animals, eager to badger newcomers, but because of Walter's connections with the mob, they steered clear of him and Perlow. He had never spent a night in jail. He refused to eat the bland food and stayed awake all night. The next day Bonnie pawned $60,000 worth of her jewelry for a measly $5,000 just to supply money for rent and groceries. Walter continued to promise Marshall that they would be out soon, but as the second night approached, Marshall noticed that Walter's command over his emotions was slipping. The curly-haired, gangly youth had reconciled himself to the prospect of at least several weeks behind bars. That prospect horrified Walter. He choked at the thought of spending one more night locked up. His optimism was fading, his flair and his spirit too.

On the second day, when the noontime meal was served, he poked a few bites in his mouth. He had gone two days without food or sleep. He gave up. He chewed the food slowly, deliberately. He pushed the spoon into his mouth for a third bite. He could not eat garbage. He spit it across the plate.

Walter met with his attorney regularly. Nothing was being accomplished for his release. After the second week, he erupted, yelling and screaming at Cockman. "When the hell am I getting out?"

"I'm working on it," Cockman responded coolly.

Walter leaped across the table and slammed Cockman against the wall. "I've got to get out, now. Damn it, get me out, now, today, do you hear me, today!" Guards pried Walter loose from his sole link to the outside world and freedom. Any future consultation would be conducted in a maximum-security room, where glass would separate him from others, jail officials mandated.

Walter's vitriolic and contempt exploded and spewed in every direction. Most of the men in the crowded cell dwarfed him, but he lashed out at them, taunted, dared, and challenged them. He rushed into the TV room and shouted, "Turn off the god damn TV or I'll break it and all of you!" Men listening to their radios at an inopportune time were blasted. "Turn that shit off, now!" he ordered.

These men for the most part were society's rejects. They could be brutal too, but each time they resisted him he warned maniacally, "When you sleep tonight, sleep light, 'cause if you don't turn that TV off, I'm gonna light the cell on fire."

The men were so spooked that they demanded the security guards place him in another cell. If things did not go his way, he would brush by an inmate, and whisper, "Don't go to sleep tonight." Marshall was the only inmate who slept. Shaw could not sleep. The other eight men dared not sleep, and neither he nor they would sleep until he went before the court for sentencing.

35

CHAPTER THIRTY-FIVE

Finally Judge Wiessing issued notice for a sentencing date. Marshall's lawyer had begged the court for mercy. His client was only a "kid." There was little mercy to be found. Marshall Perlow received thirteen years. Walter received fifteen. He was stupefied. Still convinced that he could win the original case in appeals court, he chose to fight in court a second time.

The next case, also for breaking and entering, was tried in Fort Lauderdale. The verdict was quick – guilty. Another fifteen-year sentence was heaped on. Next the state brought him up on a charge of possession and conspiracy to distribute cocaine, stemming from his run-in with the two undercover narcotics officers. He was acquitted, but the victories were hollow. He had been sentenced to thirty years for the two burglary convictions and there were other trials to come.

When the state lost its case in the possession-and-conspiracy trial, the Feds took up the slack. On September 24, 1975, in federal court, Walter was convicted of drug trafficking and handed three four-year sentences; once the twelve years were served, he would be on supervised parole from two years to life. Bonnie, who had dutifully attended each trial, upon hearing the harsh sentence, lost her composure. She wailed out like a banshee and had to be forcibly removed from court.

On the other hand, the prosecutor in the case, Kerry Nahoom, protested that the decision of Federal District Judge Norman C. Roettger, Jr. was too lenient. He tried to go over Roettger's head to get a longer sentence, and Judge Roettger held him in contempt of court.

Walter remembers that a strange twist occurred later. Nahoom, so incensed at Judge Roettger's leniency in the first case against Shaw, was himself indicted for cocaine trafficking in 1984. Perhaps more disturbing than his hypocrisy was his willful and blatant abuse of the legal system. Nahoom was never fingered for this crime. Only a few people even knew that he had betrayed his ethical obligations in practicing law.

Frank Troy, a Florida Department of Criminal Law Enforcement officer, knew, Walter Shaw knew, and The Bear knew. In 1975 Nahoom actually had two employeres who were out to get Shaw. The federal government employed Nahoom to prove Shaw's guilt in a counterfeiting case and a cocaine case. Although failing to get a conviction in the counterfeiting case, Nahoom was successful in the cocaine trial.

Nahoom's second employer, also powerful, had hired him to determine if Shaw was in fact an informant. When Nahoom stood in federal court grilling Shaw about his status as an informant, the entire courtroom full of people, including Shaw and his attorney, was being deceived. Nahoom appeared to be making an attempt to discredit Shaw as an informant, trying to prove he was not an informant at all, in order to get a conviction. Walter's attorney, Peter Aiken, in what he believed to be a clever defense ploy, fought to prove that Shaw was· an informant even though he knew he was not. He hoped to free him from a lengthy prison stay by proving that Shaw believed his actions in relation to the counterfeiting ring were a part of his position as an informant.

Nahoom's badgering served two purposes. As Walter lied and struggled to portray a deep involvement with the Florida Department of Criminal Law Enforcement, Nahoom listened carefully. No one would have suspected anything had it not been for the fact that Frank Troy, the FDCLE agent, discovered that Nahoom's second employer was none other than The Bear. More amazing still, Nahoom became The Bear's attorney after his stint as a federal prosecutor.

As Shaw boasted about his role as an informant in court to extricate himself from a counterfeiting conviction, he was actually placing his head into a noose. He would have fared better to have pleaded guilty and kept his mouth shut. Nahoom carried every word of his testimony, most of which was fallacious or exaggerated, straight to The Bear. Someone was ratting on The Bear, and the stocky mafioso wanted the rat eliminated. Walter and his attorney Aiken, performed so well in court that Judge Roettger believed them. He acquitted Shaw of the counterfeiting charges.

Later, when Walter faced cocaine charges, Roettger let it be known that Shaw's head was valued at $200,000. It became clear that someone else had been convinced of Shaw's dubious testimony too. The Bear believed his testimony, and rumor had it that the $200,000 contract was his way of saying "shut up," or actually his way of shutting up Shaw for good.

36

CHAPTER THIRTY-SIX

The unknown drama of Walter's two federal court appearances provided one of the most complex plots in law enforcement history. The story involved many important individuals, and its roots trace back to the summer of 1973, long before Shaw's convictions for burglary.

Walter's sister Linda started dating a man named Joel Leon Baker during her senior year in high school, back in the sixties. Baker and Walter became friends. A career criminal, Baker spent time in a Mississippi state prison where he learned the coveted art of printing counterfeit money. Once he was released, word of his artistic talent spread. He was commissioned by a man in New Jersey to produce several million beautiful dollars. Early in 1973 he moved back to Florida to begin his assignment. An article by Everett Harvey, staff writer for the *Hollywood Sun-Tattler*, carried the following: "After he opened his own shop, Baker testified, Shaw warned him not to print any more counterfeit money... Baker had obligations to a man in New Jersey... who was urging him to print more money. Shaw, he testified, went with him on July 6, 1974, to meet the New Jersey man. Shaw was an informer at the time, but the matter was very, very complicated ... Shaw, he said, tried to help him." Complicated, yes, but much more complicated than Baker or any of the Florida newspapers could have imagined.

Before Shaw traveled with Baker to New Jersey, he talked with FDCLE agent Frank Troy about making a deal. Troy, and nearly every FDCLE officer in south Florida, as well as agents from the United States Treasury Department, were in a panic. Baker's work was almost flawless, his twenty-dollar bills a work of art. Troy had earlier, on several occasions, approached Shaw to enlist his support as an informant. When Walter was arrested for possession of stolen-checks after being paid by Amy Stephenson for the murder contract, he had contacted Troy. He told Troy he would not rat on anyone, but he could help Troy get the counterfeit twenties off the street if Troy would get the stolen checks charge dropped. Before Troy could clear the matter, Walter learned that the case would be dismissed. Martin Stein had dropped the charges. Meanwhile he heard that Baker's investor/patron friend in New Jersey had been found dead in the trunk of his car. He wouldn't be pressuring Baker to deliver the counterfeit money.

Joel Baker immediately sought new customers. He met Nick Genitilia. In testimony Baker revealed that Genitilia, "had definite [organized crime] connections... Nick was a bad guy to cross." He also stated that Nick had told him, "Resign yourself. You're going to print some money." Shaw warned Baker not to make the deal. It was a setup. Genitilia, he had been tipped, was a government plant. Shaw had picked up the tidbit from Troy when Troy had thought he would cooperate. Shaw was warned to stay out of Genitilia's way. To deal with Genitilia was to face an indictment. An informant is not as effective in prison as he is on the streets. Baker, on the other hand, did not trust Shaw. A rumor was afloat that he was chummy with law enforcement personnel, maybe even a paid government informant.

Even had the rumor not existed, Baker's greed would have overridden caution. He started his press on a Friday night and by Sunday he had trimmed and neatly stacked over $5 million in counterfeit money. Then, after second thoughts, he decided that he would not sell to Genitilia. Later he testified that on Sunday night Walter walked into his house, "saw the money and began counting it." He told Walter that he was going to destroy the money. Shaw, he stated, objected, taking with him the bogus twenties and two cutting boards to finish the trimming. Walter was never one to let a profitable opportunity pass unexploited. He took the bills home and starched, ironed, and admired them. Very few experiences were as exhilarating as fondling over five million dollars, even if it was counterfeit.

The fun was short-lived. Baker changed his mind again. He decided to deal with Genitilia. When Baker picked up the money from Walter's house, only Bonnie was home. He did not bother to count the cash. He should have. Walter had withheld his own private stash of the bogus money totaling one million dollars.

Baker met Genitilia, offered his "art," and was promptly arrested. Walter contacted Troy and told him that Baker had hidden some of the money. He could get the rest of the bogus bills if Troy would arrange bond for Baker. Troy had already told Bill Barber, the U.S. Treasury agent working on the case, that he had collected all of the money that was on the street. Shaw's "extra" one million made him an incompetent or, worse, a liar. He instructed Walter to leave the bogus bills and the plates in a garbage dumpster. He would secure Baker's bond. Troy managed to deliver on the bond, but it came a little too late. Before the bond hearing could be scheduled, Baker rolled over on Walter, implicating him as a cog in a counterfeiting ring. The quality of the bills, combined with the amount that had been printed, inspired the United States Secret Service to call the ring the largest ever broken in the southeastern United States. Walter had put himself right in the middle.

Baker, whom he had tried to help for the sake of his sister, was a lousy bum. But ongoing dialogue with Troy had paid a dividend. He had been able to negotiate a bond for the rat. That successful negotiation might have led to other beneficial deals. What Walter did not know was that there were other players vying for parts in the unfolding drama. Frank Troy's partner, Stan Rowl, also known as Rotten Rowl, according to Walter, had a powerful informant in his stable, one who did not share Walter's scruples about being a stool pigeon. The informant, Rowl believed, was in the position to give him a lock on a man destined to be an organized crime boss, a genuine *capo*. This would be big-league crime-busting, far beyond the counterfeiting ring that had gained such a deluge of media coverage. Through his pliable informant he would put one of the nation's most notorious mobsters behind bars. The informant was none other than Pete Salerno. The prey was The Bear.

Trapping The Bear would require flawless maneuvering and a diversion. Stan Rowl knew about Shaw's exchanges with Troy. He also knew that Shaw was getting a reputation on the street as an informant. The stage was set. If Shaw could be further publicized as an informant, it would divert The Bear's attention, allowing Salerno to get closer to him. Salerno's disclosures would be blamed on Shaw. Everyone knew about Shaw's gun-wielding break with The Bear. He had a motive for doing in The Bear. Shaw was scum anyway. So what if he paid for the deception with his life? For over five years every

FDCLE agent had fantasized about being the one to nail The Bear. The Bear was top priority. If Walter fell in the hunt, who really cared? That was part of the game. Rotten Rowl was ready to play hardball.

Later, when Shaw stood before a statewide grand jury on organized crime, Rowl came forward to state that Shaw was an informant and had been one since 1973. Several articles by the *Sun-Tattler* to that same effect began to cement his reputation as an informant. The press came alive. Walter was due to face, and had faced, charges of burglary. If he had been an informant for the Florida Department of Criminal Law Enforcement since 1973, during the heaviest period of his burglary activity, then something was amiss with law enforcement agencies. Heads would roll. They did.

The *Miami Herald*, on Saturday, December 18, 1975, carried an article by Virginia Ellis which outlined a raging controversy among Florida politicians. "The chairman of the Senate Judiciary Criminal Committee Friday called on Gov. Reubin Askew and the Cabinet to investigate the ineffective management of the Florida Department of Criminal Law Enforcement. Sen. Edgar Dunn (D., Daytona Beach), Askew's legal counsel when FDCLE Director William Troelstrup was appointed, said he was concerned about certain recent decisions and actions by Troelstrup. 'I'm not condemning Bill [Troelstrup], who happens to be a friend; he just happens to be a very ineffective guy'."

Florida politicians, from Governor Askew down to state senators and finally FDCLE agents, were fighting life and limb to put out the fire. The political mud-slinging was thoroughgoing. Even a friend, as Senator Dunn stated, was called a "very ineffective guy." Surely Florida hadn't used its taxpayer's money, at the rate of $30,000 over a two-year period (the amount alleged to have been paid to Shaw), to compensate a man who was simultaneously robbing the same Florida taxpayers of everything that had not been taken from them at tax time by the state government.

Several south Florida police departments were infuriated. A rumor circulated that Shaw had been warned by FDCLE agents of police stakeouts, to prevent him from being caught. There were even allegations that Shaw was told when and where to go and not to go. In an October 2, 1985, *Sun-Tattler* article, Hollywood Police Chief Sam Martin was quoted as saying of the FDCLE's alleged protection of Shaw that he "didn't know it then, but know[s] it now . . . My initial reaction made me sick . . . It shocks us and makes us mad to find out when you're working with other agencies that the suspect you have is working for them."

Walter Shaw suddenly became hot copy. He was unknown because he was good. The best thief is the one who doesn't get caught by either the police or the newspapers. At first, he appeared to be just another hood. But the real story slowly unfolded. The *Miami Herald* ran a full-page feature article on Sunday, October 26, 1975. Under three titles – "Informant: Major Criminal or Minor Hood?"; "Walter Shaw: Big Criminal, Small-Time Hood?"; and "Walter Shaw: Big Shot, or Small-Time Hood?" – writer Robert Liss described Shaw as "free-wheeling, fancy dressing. Walter Shaw . . . was driving a Lincoln Continental, had made a down payment on a Ferrari, owned 40 pairs of expensive shoes, and lived with his wife and two children in a lavish, marble floored, $150,000 golf course home in an exclusive Hollywood subdivision."

On April 26, 1975, the *Hollywood Sun-Tattler* reported that Shaw "displayed signs of affluence and success through ownership of an expensive home and several expensive cars, including reports that one of them was a Rolls Royce, while being unemployed . . . his police record dates to 1967 . . . no convictions until this year . . . police in three counties suspect Shaw to be part of a 10-year-old organized multi-million dollar ring which had burglarized thousands of homes throughout Dade, Broward and Palm Beach counties." On November 7, 1975, the *Sun-Tattler* carried these comments by Everett Harvey "While Shaw was on the FDCLE payroll, he was racking up a reputation as a leader of a burglary ring that burglarized thousands of homes in three counties of hundreds of thousands of dollars in cash and stolen property. Hollywood police said earlier this year the ring had 'organized crime' connections in New York."

At Shaw's sentencing hearing, on September 24, 1975, Federal District Court Judge Norman C. Roettger, Jr., said that Shaw was "a twentieth-century highwayman and a modern-day Jesse James."

The *Sun-Tattler* also honored Shaw by selecting him as one of the top "Newsmakers of 1975." Not to be outdone, The *Miami Herald*, quoted Judge Roettger as having titled Shaw a "Jesse James, for his multifaceted life of crime."

Newspapers from the Keys to the Panhandle were discovering this boisterous, high-living, "Walking who's who of organized crime."

Walter's face, sometimes thick and nasty, other times lean and good-looking, was pasted under eye-catching headlines across Florida. The publicity led to serious consequences. First, in Florida's Capitol, the governor and state legislators busily pointed fingers. Second, the revamping of the informant program run by the FDCLE, was initiated, and finally, Walter Shaw had become some sort of a celebrity. Shaw, it seemed for a while, was causing the legal and law enforcement structures of the State of Florida to shake, not to mention embarrassment to several elected officials. But the most dire consequence of the media blitz flowed toward Walter personally. Although

Walter's role as an informant was exaggerated, although he never participated as the newspapers claimed, it was too late to stop a reprisal from the kingpins of organized crime. Stool pigeons had to be stopped, permanently.

In an effort to escape a prison stay, strictly as a defensive measure, Shaw had lied, he says now. He told a jury he was an informant. He should not have lied. Imprisonment is better than death. A high-echelon mafioso put out a contract on his life.

When Walter faced federal charges of counterfeiting, his attorney, Peter Aiken, as stated earlier, suggested he use the media story about his being an informant to his advantage. Shaw had appeared as a secret witness before a statewide grand jury on organized crime. Eugene Whitworth, the fiery prosecutor, pushed Shaw to talk about The Bear, specifically his connection with Jimmy Hoffa's disappearance. Shaw wouldn't budge. The foreman at the trial leaked Shaw's name with the expectation that he would talk if he felt he had nothing to lose. The foreman later issued a statement admonishing the press for disclosing Shaw's identity. This superficial gesture did nothing more than generate added publicity.

Later, when Shaw was brought before Judge Roettger, Peter Aiken had Walter admit to being an informant and claim that his involvement in the alleged cocaine sale was as an informant. Aiken, an astute criminal attorney, fouled badly. Walter perpetrated the informant myth to extricate himself from a drug charge. In doing so, he sealed his reputation as a stool pigeon. He also lost the case. The move was the most costly he had ever made. Nahoom, the prosecutor in the case, as pointed out earlier, had been hired by The Bear.

Agent Frank Troy saw The Bear and Nahoom whispering over lunch one afternoon. Nahoom was directed, via the cases against Shaw, to determine if Walter was indeed an informant and if so, find out what he knew. Nahoom carried the act forward without blushing. He pushed Walter to the wall during the trial, seeking to squeeze out information about Walter's role as an informant. He called Agent Frank Troy to the stand, trying to solicit information. When Troy refused, Nahoom asked that he be found in contempt of court. The *Hollywood Sun-Tattler* wrote, "Special agent Frank Troy, an eight-year veteran of the Florida Department of Law Enforcement (FDCLE), was declared in contempt of court for refusing to identity 'M-231' as Shaw's paid-informant number."

The "eight-year veteran" knew that Nahoom was working as a double agent – the government's prosecutor and The Bear's hand-picked man. Troy refused to be a part of the lynch mob. After he had been sworn in as a defense witness, he would not acknowledge that Shaw was informant number M-231. He knew such information would guarantee Shaw a death penalty. He stated in testimony, "With all due respect to the court, I cannot answer that." Judge Roettger told Troy that he would be notified at a later date of his decision on the contempt motion. In spite of Troy's valiant efforts to undo a grievance of justice in which he alone knew the exact details, excluding Nahoom and The Bear, Walter had already been selected for termination.

The United States Government, although not privy to what Troy knew, must have assumed that there might be an attempt to retaliate against Shaw. The *Sun-Tattler* reported that "the usual compliment of two deputy U.S. Marshals used to escort defendants back to Broward County Jail was beefed up with the addition of two unidentified 'security agents' assigned to protect Shaw. After he was permitted a fifteen-minute visit with his wife in the U.S. Marshal's office in the courthouse, a deputy U.S. Marshal ran out the back door and opened the government's car door before Shaw was permitted to leave the building."

Rowl, the FDCLE agent who wanted Shaw publicized as an informant, had succeeded. The Bear was distracted, and Salerno slipped into his trust unnoticed. Nahoom went into private practice after the counterfeiting case. One of his first official clients, of course, was The Bear. Frank Troy transferred from the streets to a teaching position at the police academy, disillusioned and disgusted over the whole affair. Aiken's strategy failed, but Walter kept him on for the counterfeiting charge.

Aiken was finally successful, Walter was acquitted. But after long months, trial after trial, testimony after testimony, motion after motion, and both convictions and acquittals, Walter Thiel Shaw, Jr., was a broken young man. Now he faced something far worse than prison. He faced death. As mentioned before, Roettger let it be known that Shaw carried a $200,000 price on his head. The news shook the courtroom. The skeptics stood corrected. The only real authority on the Mafia, the Mafia itself, had cleared the air about Shaw's importance. Evidently organized crime believed that Shaw was big enough to warrant a $200,000 murder bid. Roettger continued to provide Shaw with good press. He stated that he had never, in all his years of experience, encountered a more colorful character than Shaw.

37

CHAPTER THIRTY-SEVEN

Shaw had neither the time nor the energy to enjoy such publicity. History was repeating itself. Once again, he was rewarded too late. The Bear's tag "the Crazy Kid" was uninspiring because Walter had lost his edge by the time The Bear had given him the name. Then Judge Roettger decided that he was a Jesse James. He might as well have called him Pinocchio. A "twentieth-century Jesse James" behind bars? It was a sick joke. He faced years of prison. But there was something worse. He might not get to serve one day. The sum of $200,000 would go to the first man to kill him.

In the next months he finished the last of his burglary trials. He went down again. Seven more years in prison were added. After six trials his record was two wins and four losses, big losses, losses amounting to forty-nine years of incarceration. He needed a computer to keep the numbers straight. He was confused. He had not ratted on anyone. Why would there be a murder contract on his life? As he tried to unravel the mystery behind the contract, he was hit with yet another jolt.

His father lay in a New Jersey hospital fighting for his life after a massive heart attack. He wanted to help his dad. Not since he was a boy had he felt such a strong emotional tie to him. Had it come too late? Time would tell, long, hard time, if any time at all.

The fact that Walter had become persona non grata with the mob was evidenced as soon as he was placed in the Fort Lauderdale Prison Annex. He occupied a cell with Marshall Perlow. In the evenings, when he walked past the other cells to shower, inmates threw cups of urine on him and shouted, "Stool pigeon." Night after night Walter washed the sticky urine off of his face and body and scrubbed the foul smell out of his hair.

Bonnie visited him daily. He didn't tell her about the evening baptisms. He observed that with each visit she seemed stronger. Perhaps strength was what he wanted to see. She had accepted Walter's imprisonment, but she was convinced that it was a temporary condition. Clinging to his promise that when he got out he would walk the straight and narrow, she believed he had finally learned his lesson. She encouraged him, forced weak smiles on her face: "You'll get out, don't worry."

"Yeah, I'll get out, baby." His emotional stress was accompanied by physical decay. Once – *nearly six feet, at least 170 pounds, muscular, lean, good-looking, dazzling brown eyes, sly smile, sharp dresser, so confident, outrageous, funny, fun and exciting, a dreamer.* But urine showers do not a playboy make. Bonnie's husband was a different man – *Maybe five-eleven, couldn't be 150 pounds, skinny, ratty-looking, sunken eyes, pale, white as a ghost, like a bedsheet had been pasted to his face, never smiles, never talks. Looks like he'll die, unshaved, unkempt, smelly, and dirty. A loser.*

At ten o'clock one morning he awaited Bonnie's visit. In her place in the visitor's room stood an FBI agent. The agent, grave and businesslike, told him that the government wanted to take his wife and children to a place of hiding because of the contract on his life. Later, a U.S. marshal instructed Walter that it would be wise to put his family under the marshall plan. (The marshall plan is a form of witness protection whereby the witness and his/her family are given new identities, homes, and lives.)

Walter rejected the government's idea. Placing Bonnie and his children under the protective auspices of the government would further confirm the rumor that he was an informant. Equally critical, he was emotionally incapable of doing without Bonnie. He had to have her. Since Walter refused to cooperate, prison officials were in a dilemma. Now they had the almost impossible task of keeping Walter and his family alive in broad daylight. For one of the few times the fierce competition between state and federal agencies subsided. Both had a vested interest in keeping Walter alive. It was decided that in this case the state had the best chance to meet the objective.

38

CHAPTER THIRTY-EIGHT

Walter's stay at the Fort Lauderdale annex was cut short. A young trusty, who admired him, had been tipped that ground chunks of glass had been stirred into Walter's meal for added seasoning. Some of the inmates, bored with their urine-drenching rituals, wanted Walter dead. Besides, $200,000 went to the first man or men who killed him, not humiliated him. Walter reported the ground-glass attempt to prison officials. Mandated to keep him alive, they made arrangements to move him to safer quarters. At four the next morning guards woke him, "Time to go, Shaw, grab your stuff."

Three FDCLE agents, ironically headed by Stan Rowl, and all toting submachine guns, secretly ferreted him by automobile to the Arcadia County Jail, in isolated DeSoto County, and placed him in "deep freeze" on the first floor. Marshall was left back at the annex. FDCLE wanted to keep everything in files only reviewed by selected prison personnel. They had a better chance of keeping him alive if he were alone and his location known only to a few. Arcadia was an inconspicuous jail. The early-morning move, the solitary confinement, along with the high security of the transfer, gave the FDCLE a little edge. But they were up against insurmountable odds. Not only were they fighting the far-reaching tentacles of organized crime, they now confronted another sobering development. Walter needed to be protected from himself.

He refused to eat, shave, or speak to anyone. The ground-glass incident did not frighten him, it destroyed him, the last straw in a mountainous pile of adverse events. He had existed on the verge of collapse before the first attempt on his life, even before the first warm splat of urine struck his face. In fact, he had been fading since his break with The Bear. The series of court battles merely intensified an already existent process. He often wondered what he would have done if he had not gone to prison. It was that question which haunted him, and his inability to provide a suitable answer which weakened him.

Actually, he had been a prisoner for many years, at first unknowingly. He had been on a journey of expanded consciousness, of revelation, each year learning more and more of the truth. He was a slave. A victim. Owned. By what he did not know. He did recognize, however, that even the "good old days," before his split with The Bear, had been a state of stupidity. The deepest longing of every inmate, that which keeps him alive, is his hope to get out one way or another. Walter was not sustained with such hope. There were moments when he did not care whether he served two months or twenty years. There was no escape from the truth of his existence. He worried about hanging on for forty-nine years. He wanted to survive for Bonnie's sake, he reasoned, but that was no good either. How would Bonnie make it? Would she wait patiently for over half of her life, like Dostoevsky's Sonya, enduring grief she did not deserve? Should he allow her to wait and suffer in the vast expanse of loneliness, a psychological Siberia? He knew neither Dostoevsky nor his Sonya, but he understood something of separation and abject loneliness. He knew there would be no appeals, reversals, or gifts.

There was one answer. It presented itself in a dignified and unpresupposing way at first. It did not prod, it merely introduced itself. When he wished it away, it left *almost* entirely. He said good-bye to this visiting thought, not quite his, with a "Not yet, I can't . . . not yet."

Soon, he drifted into chaos. Marshall Perlow was transferred to Arcadia in an effort to help Walter grab hold. Bonnie moved to Arcadia to be closer to him also. On one of her visits he told her, tears moving down his cheeks, not to bring the children anymore. "They keep asking me to go home with them, I can't take it. It's making me crazy."

To hold on financially, Bonnie was forced to sell all remaining jewelry and the extra car. She worked in Arcadia for the Department of Health and Rehabilitative Services as a secretary. Shortly after the transfer to Arcadia, Walter Sr. recovered from his heart attack and began to send Bonnie as much money as he could afford. John Donaldson, living up to his promise, aided Bonnie and Walter's two children as well. Walter saw Bonnie deteriorating a little more with each visit. He had thought she was growing stronger, but now it seemed the optimism was evaporating. She looked ten years older, in two months aging ten years. What had made him think she was growing stronger? He must have imagined it.

Their conversations were redundant. Walter asked her the same questions twice, even three times, and more, not out of insecurity but out of loss, loss of mind. He could not remember from one minute to the next what he had said. He could not recall what he wanted to say either. He thought about what he would say to Bonnie, went over it in his mind. She arrived and he went blank. Prison doctors kept him sedated, twenty milligrams of Valium in the morning and twenty in the afternoon. The heavy doses increased the incoherence. He began to fade out.

During December his mother and father came down from New Jersey. Walter Sr. had lost his business, and as he walked into the Arcadia County Jail, he lamented that he was incapable of helping his son.

Each cell was fourteen feet by fourteen feet. Walter Sr. was no stranger to such an environment. He knew exactly what his son was experiencing. When he spotted Walter, he wept. "Don't worry, we'll get you out," he said, knowing he lacked the financial resources to fulfill the promise. Walter's mother cried too. What could his father do? He was barely alive after the massive heart attack and he had no steady source of income. He needed help himself. "By God, I'll get you out," he sobbed anyway.

Walter's mind wandered. "Last year I spent nearly $5,000 on my children for Christmas, went out Christmas Eve and got drunk, didn't get back till morning. But five grand I spent. That was something. This year I ain't gonna be home either. But no five-grand Christmas. They don't have a dime – I don't have nothing to give them, not even a card."

"Oh Walter, your father and I will help," began his mother.

Walter Sr. interrupted "Son, we're gonna get Bonnie taken care of and get you out. It'll be just like in '69 with everyone all together." Dazed, he had not even heard his wife speak.

"It'll be good then, Dad . . . thank you." Walter went back to his cell and fell back on his bunk.

"Hey, Marshall, have you noticed that all I do is bring people trouble?" asked Walter.

"No," responded Marshall, bracing for Walter's next statement.

"It's true, I've made Bonnie's life hell, pure hell, and my

mother and father just left crying. I mean they are suffering because of me. I've disappointed the shit out of my father forever. Disappear! That's the best thing I could do for everyone," he dragged on.

"Get some sleep, Walt," Perlow responded.

Shaw thought about a solution for several days. A single answer came to him frequently. Still dignified but now more determined, more passionate. After several days the answer lost all dignity. It had become his idea and whatever became part of him lacked dignity. His answer it was. Driving, relentless, it would not leave. One night he turned to Marshall and bluntly stated, "You know, we're not getting out of here."

"No, we'll get out," Marshall said in his usual carefree tone.

"I'm not," Walter whispered.

At one the next morning, he committed himself to the thought that had become so powerful. He called it a soldier's death. He refused to die at the hands of another person. In death perhaps he could give, stop being a taker. If he were gone, it would relieve Bonnie, his children, and his parents from the pain he had caused and would continue to cause. He would die anyway. What he presumed to be The Bear's $200,000 contract had motivated every freak, bad man, and calculated killer in the world to destroy him. He sat in prison, right in the middle of the most dangerous of men, without a chance. This way, his way, he could give. A soldier's death, as Walter understood it, was suicide by drowning. He sat up. He didn't have a bathtub. The sink wasn't deep enough. He'd have to make do with a flat-floored shower stall. Perlow, dozing, jerked up and saw him sitting on the edge of his bed. "Walt, what's goin' on? Why are you up?" he asked.

"Nothing, I'm going to bed. Just go back to sleep," he said. After a deep breath Walter lay back down and slipped into a light sleep.

39

CHAPTER THIRTY-NINE

Walter slept less than two hours. He opened his eyes and looked at his watch. 3:00 A.M. Marshall would not be stirring for the rest of the night. It was December 14, 1975 and it was cold, very cold. Snores were the only sound that could be heard. The county jail was a chamber of snores. He wrapped his bedsheet and blanket around his shoulders and walked into the shower area. The lip on the floor of the shower, which kept water from running into the cell, stood about one foot high. Everything was relatively clean because the Arcadia County Jail was only two years old. The beige-tiled bath facility had two stainless-steel buttons for hot and cold water. The shower stall itself looked sterile. The bathroom was much darker than the pale white cell. Compared to the milky color of the cell walls even beige became an abyss in the night. Walter had not had a change of clothing since being locked up in Fort Lauderdale. Only matriculated convicts received prison-issue clothes. He wore a wrinkled pair of $125 Jupiter of Paris gray slacks, black silk socks, a pair of hundred-dollar Florsheim leather loafers, and an eighty-dollar Merkesh light-blue silk shirt. He had been sleeping in his clothes since his first night behind bars. Without jewelry, unshaved for weeks, his hair was long, he was emaciated. All power was gone.

The most dramatic and grandiose act of his life was unfolding. The forthcoming episode was not performed in rage, or sorrow, or passion. If there is one neutral moment in life, one empty-headed, clear moment, it is that moment before suicide. To take a life requires a reversal of all that is human. It requires a spiritual death that manifests itself in a choking neutrality. T.S. Eliot's poem "The Hollow Men" describes a civilization of suicidal men. Those lines, changed here to apply to one man, cannot be improved upon to describe the lonely man who forfeits his life.

He is the hollow man

He is the stuffed man

Headpiece filled with straw

Walter reached up for his razor. The clean blade had never been used. He did not think about Bonnie, his mother, his father, good times or bad. He did not think at all. His movements were graceful – catlike. He used all his skills to negotiate this, his greatest theft, his final theft. Stooping down and quietly tearing two long strips from the white bedsheet, he eased the gray Arcadia County Jail blanket from his back. He rested for a moment, free at last from all passion and confusion.

Remember him – if at all – not as a lost

Violent soul, but only

As the hollow man

He took one strip with his mouth and free hand, and tied it above his elbow. He repeated the process on his other arm, mindlessly. The makeshift tourniquets in place, he tightened them – mindlessly.

Shape without form, shade without color,

Paralyzed force, gesture without motion;

With his shirtsleeves pulled up tight around his arms, the tourniquets much tighter, blood rushed to dizzy his limbs. A flash, a thought . . . *They will be better off without me.* He wanted, one last time, to love. *I would love tenderly now . . . speak respectfully now.* He would have done anything to love someone . . . now.

It is like this

In death's other kingdom

Waking alone

At the hour when he is

Trembling with tenderness

Lips that would kiss

Form prayers to broken stone

He pinched the Wilkerson razor blade between his thumb and index finger positioning his forearm on the lip of the shower. He leaned on it heavily to make sure that the arm was deadened. No sense in causing extra pain. He made a fist, squeezed, realized his mind was blank, and slashed at the wrist wildly. His effort produced a small crimson trickle. He had hit too high – almost the palm of his hand.

> *Between the motion*
>
> *And the act*
>
> *Falls the Shadow*

Another chance, another moment, to finish. Determined, he struck out once more. He failed, too close to his hand again. This agitated him, filled him with indignation and a trite suicidal thought: *Can't I do anything right?* Aggravated that his course required conscious effort, he placed the blade purposefully, mindfully, onto his wrist. Then – he dragged...down. The blade dug deep. He looked up when he heard it scrape the bone and back down when it popped out of his flesh. Nothing happened for a half-second. An eternity . . .

> *Between the conception*
>
> *And the creation*
>
> *Between the emotion*
>
> *And the response*
>
> *Falls the Shadow*
>
> *Life is very long*

But the blood did gush forth. It shot up like an angry geyser as if to say, *Now you have me*. It flowed into the air, arched and splattered over the lip into the cell. The tourniquet was ineffective. The pain became wrenching, laughing at him. It surprised him. There was little time. He had to proceed. Soon he would lose the use of his left arm. He placed the blade between his thumb and index finger again, tried to squeeze, but his strength was leaving. He knew he would only get one slash, so he slashed slow and hard.

Blood spurted up but not as high as the first time. He did not scrape the bone of his right arm. The blade fell and he sat back against the cold tile of the stall. The fountain like spurting died quickly, but with every heartbeat a thick gush would surface. He could hear each beat, the thud of his heart was like a hammer pounding. He was cold and reached out to pull the blanket around him, but it hurt to grab. He felt millions of needles jabbing into his flesh. He managed to get the blanket around him somehow, but it was the warm blood that fended off the cold. He was covered in it. It had soaked through his shirt and pants. It was no small comfort, though it was sticky. He saw flashing black and silver dots, tiny atoms, and grew light-headed.

Leaning his throbbing head into the corner of the shower, feeling warm then cold, and sticky, he closed his eyes for a minute. This was the first relaxation he had had since prison. *I am so tired.* He hadn't been honest in a long time. He had never been honest with himself. *This really is the best thing.* He took one last mind's-eye glance at his family, his parents, and his life. *I give up, just let me sleep . . .*

Walter Thiel Shaw, Jr., – Dinnertime Burglar, hit man, con man, wild man, killer, freewheeler, dazzler, joker, and "Crazy Kid" – drained away. For all of his passion, this Jesse James was empty and lifeless. This man of action was a hollow man, a stuffed man. No parades or gasps, no screams or salutes, just a weary, dying, young man – sunken eyes closed.

This is the way life ends

This is the way life ends

This is the way life ends

Not with a bang but a whimper.

40

CHAPTER FORTY

"Walter, what the hell are you doing?" Marshall's voice sounded six blocks away. Walter squinted. He tried to peer through the bright light, then opened his mouth to speak. Words failed to form. "Why are you in the shower with a blanket? Walt, wake up . . . Oh God!" Marshall screamed out. The gray blanket was blood soaked.

Walter scrunched his face into an angry scowl. "Stay out!" he ordered.

"I can't, Walt." Marshall ran from the shower to call a guard. When the guard got there, he buckled, his heart almost stopping. Blood was everywhere, the blanket was solid red, and Walter was mumbling reprimands like a senile old man. When the paramedics arrived, they stuck assorted needles into Walter's limp body. He maintained consciousness as they put him on the stretcher, but once in the ambulance he blacked out.

When he came to he noticed that a tight bandage had been wrapped around his left arm. A needle pushed and pulled in and out of his other arm. Someone was sewing him up. He blacked out again and came to several minutes later. A doctor leaned over the bed, and stared into his eyes. "Next time you want to kill yourself, put the blade here," he said, patting the jugular vein on Walter's neck. "That way there'll be nothing we can do to save you," he finished with a harsh laugh.

"I'll try and remember that," Walter whispered.

He had failed. That was obvious.

After the hospital recuperation, he was returned to Arcadia to be placed in isolation two cells down from Marshall. The cell was bare, no blanket, mattress, personals, or even toilet tissue. Any object might be fashioned into a suicide aide. The cell was shut tight. A steel door allowed no outside light. Walter was too tired to care. For weeks his arms ached intensely, then slowly the pain subsided. Though he slept twelve to sixteen hours each day, he was exhausted. Every two days he was taken out to be shaved. He could hardly lift his arm and gripping a razor was out of the question. Thick bandages covered his forearms.

Later, Bonnie and his mother were allowed to visit. He wore a long-sleeved shirt to hide the bandages, but when he put his arms clumsily around Bonnie, she could feel them. She and his mother cried. He cried a little, and promised he wouldn't try it again. "I'll just let them kill me slowly, day after day."

Walter's suicide attempt did not solicit compassion from the architect of the $200,000 murder contract, or from greedy henchmen who hoped to collect the prize. Walter transferred from Arcadia to the Tarpon Springs Work Release Center as soon as doctors agreed that he could handle the move. He was placed in solitary confinement. The chief left him with a brief message: "Don't get used to the place – you're not staying."

Bonnie followed him to Tampa. She explained that she wouldn't be able to see him for a while because she had been told he was going "into the system." This meant the beginning of hard time.

Lieutenant Ray Henderson, a special roving classification

specialist from the Department of Corrections at Tallahassee, transported Walter from Tarpon Springs to North Sumter Correctional Institute on January 28, 1976, just one day after his birthday. He was not going "into the system." That was a cover-up. Sumter Correctional Institute housed 1,500 men, and was complete with gun towers. The rank and file of Sumter prison officials read documents indicating that their new inmate was named John Simms. John, because of his tuberculosis, would be staying in a hospital wing isolation cell. His room had a bed, a sink, a window, and a solid oak door. First-class. The superintendent informed him that he alone knew his identity. "To everyone else you're John Simms." Then he added, "And to keep that glass out of your food two of my men will feed you . . . no one else."

Bonnie was allowed to visit, the only person permitted to do so. Even his parents were kept in the dark. Each night at nine he was given one approved phone call. Aside from Bonnie's visits, his nightly calls, and the two lieutenants who brought him his meals, he had no contact with other people. He spent most of his time sleeping. His conscious hours were torturous. The solitude began to fester inside him again.

Bonnie's company wasn't always positive either. The realization of the magnitude of the destruction Walter had caused her began to flare up. She was stuck with two kids and a high school diploma. She had begged him to break from crime, but he never did. As if that weren't bad enough, he treated her like an unwanted but necessary possession, like an old heirloom, valuable in some way, but stuck in a drawer. She had endured one blatant affair of his after another. He would come home night after night, energy spent elsewhere, without the strength or inclination to love her. There were many women who got the best of Walter – his money, laughs, attention, and intimacy. Bonnie lived with the mess that was his life, arrogance, irresponsibility, insensitivity, and callousness. Driven by something she could neither describe nor understand, he ruined everything that was good. She had to raise and care for his two kids. She had to explain what their daddy did for a living. She had to sit up nights wondering if he would come home – not nights when he was out with a woman, those nights were easy, he'd always come home from a date. But what about the burglaries, the power plays? Would he come home from them, or would he end up like Bill Marlow?

When Walter was indicted, Bonnie dragged her children from courtroom to courtroom. She bled for him, died each time a judge handed him more time, and exhausted herself trying to give him hope when there was none. Forty-nine years! Who was really the prisoner? Walter? Hah! She sold everything she had ever owned. Sold every car. Every house. Every stick of furniture. At twenty-five she was flat broke with two hungry children and a husband in prison.

The suicide attempt topped it all. Who in the hell did he think he was? "God damn him!" Did he think he had a right to just cut out? He courted and married her. He fathered their children. He dragged her up and down the pits of hell. Suicide? It was so typical of Walter Shaw, so typically selfish and egocentric, so typically cowardly and grandstandish, so typically "I don't give a damn about anyone else but myself, and let's see who I can make feel sorry for me when I die." Had she tried? Night after day after night she tried until *she* failed because *he* ended up in prison. Now she would be forced to serve forty-nine years along with him. Even if he got out tomorrow, what good would it do? He would never stop committing crimes. He was too weak and too egotistical. He had to be a big shot.

The crime arena is a stage for such men. Insecure, selfish babies who show strength by collecting and breaking toys –

toys, meaning people and things. The more toys collected and broken, the tougher the man, or in reality, the bigger the baby. Unfortunately, the crime syndicate and all the other burglars, rapists, extortionists, pornographers, and killers in the world don't practice their trade in playpens. Nor do they reserve their ambitions to plastic toys. Human beings fall into the hands of these emotional, mental, and spiritual retards, and they are not mature enough to know how to live with something as precious as a human life. Bonnie had lived with an emotional, mental, and spiritual retard all her adult life. Still, she continued to reach out, to try and to hope. She loved him.

41

CHAPTER FORTY-ONE

Observing Walter's unchanging, downward mood, the superintendent at North Sumter decided that Walter could not handle solitary confinement. Prison officials were in an awkward position. If they placed him "in population," he would be dead in a matter of days if not hours. Keeping him in solitary opened the possibility of another suicide attempt. All things considered, after seeing him bug out day after day, witnessing a twenty-eight-year-old becoming a crazy old man, the officials decided that he had to be integrated with other inmates. A prison far removed from the hustle of big-time crime might provide safety in population. It was a gamble they had to take. He was shipped to the Lake City Correctional Institute.

At Lake City he was one of eighty men to a dorm. Several days after the move a guard overheard three inmates plotting his demise. Even in the country he had been recognized. Officials quickly transferred him to the Tavares County Jail. He spent one week there. Even Bonnie did not know his whereabouts. He had become a prison road show, moving from one location to another. From Tavares he was sent to Brevard County's correctional institution. The withdrawal symptoms persisted.

Men form unusual habits in prison. Denied freedom, they are stuck in an environment that is either clean to the point of sterility or so filthy it is degrading. It is an environment of extremes. Everything is painted the same color, whatever that color may be – the same geometrical shapes, no curves or free lines, only rigid squares and rectangles. If a prison is clean, it is impersonal and alienating. If it is dirty, it is tormenting and draining. Prison is a place to think. There is little else to do. Men physically hang over structures – chairs, prison bars, beds, slouching like half-empty bags of feed until they are forced to think. Most prisoners have either never thought before or, if they have used their minds, they did so incorrectly. Consequently, prison becomes a perverted think-tank, a place full of twisted, dangerous, futile thoughts. Bad thinking is passed around from inmate to inmate, thus they share unwittingly in each other's mental demise, feeding negativity from cell to cell like a virus.

Walter had always been a thinker of sorts. Not a thorough thinker, but nevertheless a clever one. He had never had time to think too thoroughly. He shot from the hip and often hit the target instinctually. In prison he began to think things out, to reach conclusions. Energy was coming back. As tired as he was, as hopeless as his status was, as futile and empty as his life might seem, he could still resurrect his drive. First he had to decide if he wanted to live or not, a decision that was still unresolved. Like other inmates, he was going through peculiar mental machinations. One minute he plotted a murder and the next he contemplated another try at suicide. Extremes, it would be one or the other. Either way, someone would pay for his unhappiness.

Bonnie, now informed of his location, visited Walter faithfully. They never talked about anything substantive. She quit trying to communicate with him. They spoke a language of slogan and ideology. Their slogan was "Don't give up," their ideology the distant and dying love that they felt for one another. Walter knew little about her. He never had, really. From the beginning she had chosen not to talk about herself, her deepest thoughts and feelings, and he was too wrapped up in himself to care. After imprisonment, he began to want to know, but how could he go about it? Now, the lack of knowing nagged at him. She started bringing his children to visit again again, believing it would help him, despite his protests to the contrary. In any case, they needed to see their father. On each visit they walked to the visiting park and did the best they could to understand each other.

Much had changed in Bonnie's life. The visits were difficult. Her love for Walter, a love she had protected for so long, had nourished against every odd, was weakening as her resentment increased. She was weary. It seemed to her that Walter had been in prison forever.

"How is Mommy doing, Randy?" Walter asked his six-year-old son on one visit. "You have to be the man of the house while Daddy's gone." His son did not respond. "Do you sleep with Mommy to protect her?" he tried again.

"No," his son answered, now hostile.

"Why not?" Walter asked kindly.

"Because Mommy sleeps with a man."

Bonnie had taken Shelley to the restroom. When she saw Walter's face, she whispered, "I knew I shouldn't have left him out here."

"I want to talk, alone," Walter said. Bonnie's eyes were fixed on the ground. She let go of Shelley's hand and stood silently. The children walked away. "Is it true?" Walter asked.

"He's my boss and I . . ." Bonnie began to explain, but Walter interrupted her.

"Do you love him?" he asked. She didn't answer. He closed his eyes and then placed his hands over his face for a few seconds. He was not prepared for his son's innocent revelation. Bonnie had never cheated on him before.

Bonnie finally spoke. "I love you." She remembered when she had first met him. He had energy and charisma. He was a fighter, hot and cold, a source of inexhaustible fascination and intrigue. He always dreamed big enough for two. Then he quit dreaming. He loved her dearly once. To prove it, he had held a gun to one of the Mafia's biggest men. He used to be proud of her.

"DO YOU LOVE HIM?" he demanded.

"I DON'T KNOW," she cried out.

He slapped her. It was a quick, painful blow. "You're sleeping with some fat cowboy slob and you don't know!" He bellowed as she grabbed her two children and ran.

"You don't know?" he screamed again. She rushed passed the prison chaplain, looked him in the eyes, and yelled, "God, get me away from him, he's an animal, he's an animal!" She fled down the hall, out of the prison, and into her car. Walter, alone, screamed out once more, "You don't know?"

A curious thing happened after he slapped her. Now he was glad he had not died. Being alive gave him the opportunity to feel her betrayal and then to punish her for it. He wanted to strike her again and again and again until she admitted something, anything, perhaps that she was to blame for his misery. "Damn her!" He had nearly killed himself while she was sleeping around. He kicked, dragged his hands across his unshaved face, and gasped for air. The intense anger shifted to pain. He withdrew even more deeply within himself. He sat motionless. An image of Bonnie and her employer making love flashed in his mind. It came from nowhere, suddenly attacking. It sickened him, tormented him, then stimulated him. He wanted to have her. Knowing that someone else had made love to her only intensified his desire. He burned with lust, toyed with Bonnie and her cowboy lover, inflicted pain on her through him, used her through him, ravaged her through him, spent himself, and finally, revolted, he sat crying. "My God, I'm going crazy."

He was certainly not a saint, but he never had thoughts like that before. These mental games were sick, "crazy sick." "I do love her," he promised, and cried harder and harder trying to cleanse himself of the evil ritual that had just transpired. "What's happening to me?" He resolved to never think such thoughts again.

It was a decisive moment. Throughout his past, every reprehensible act he had ever committed was uncalculated. His thefts, his beatings, his threats, were all rather shallow actions. He was motivated by two things at first. Money – he wanted luxury – and pride – he wanted to be famous, to be liked. Every move that he made was a staged performance, an attention-getter. After The Bear hit on his wife, he entered a new phase. His motivation was a deep and profound unrest, and all of his actions were violent lashings at an unseen force which he blamed for his trauma. In prison his strange antics turned to angry reactions, to maliciously conceived evil. He wanted to cause people pain for the sake of pain. His suicidal streak had been replaced by a desire to brutalize, to hurt.

He had been brutal before, but the incidents in the past paled in comparison to what he now planned. He wanted revenge for his prison stay; revenge for the glass in his food; revenge for his wife's infidelity; revenge for the suicide attempt, the isolation, the dread, the loneliness; revenge for the bum rap of being a stool pigeon. Revenge. Revenge. Revenge!

He wanted it. Whether it was the full forty-nine years, or just a few, his anger would have its day.

He imagined it would be pleasurable. He plotted hundreds of criminal acts for revenge, to pay back someone, anyone, the system, the world. But at last, the energizing drive toward revenge transformed itself into another monster. In the end he was sadistic. He wept knowing he was rushing headlong down a path with no place to turn around. He was becoming evil. No longer himself, tears were wasted. They did not cleanse him. Out of his suicide, near death, a new man had arisen. If the old Walter did not want to live, the new one did. The new Walter Shaw was not tired of life; the new Walter was growing exuberant, enthusiastic, and anxious. The old Walter asserted himself at times, but his presence no longer dominated. This strange phenomenon was a survival instinct. Maybe he had no choice except to lose himself in maliciousness. One thing was certain, he was no longer the same.

In April of 1976, Walter was put in Lake Butler's K-Wing lock-up, a scaled-down version of Death Row. Several weeks later Bonnie told Walter that she was "tired of driving all over the state just to visit once a week." He was surprised she still talked to him at all. After all that had happened between them, he still needed her. He could not face himself alone. He asked Lake Butler's Superintendent Godwin about the possibility of transferring to DeSoto County so he could be near Bonnie. Godwin advised him to let her go. He refused. Godwin then informed him that if he insisted on the transfer, it would be at his own risk, and he would be placed in population without protection. Walter agreed to the terms. To be near Bonnie, he was prepared to take the risk. She was seeing another guy. He had lost her love, her faithfulness. He could not lose seeing her.

He entered DeSoto Correctional Institute under his real name. On the second day an inmate swung at him with a huge metal pipe. The heat was still on. He shared a concrete-box confinement cell with Ricky Miller and Albert Bradshaw. Miller was scheduled to be placed in a psychiatric ward as soon as room could be found. The concrete cell contained mattresses, a toilet, and a sink. Miller and Bradshaw screamed and yelled incoherently throughout the day and most of the night. They had lost touch. To compensate for their behavior, Walter fell deeper into himself.

One day Miller and Bradshaw turned on him. They had heard about the $200,000 contract. Miller wrapped a T-shirt around Walter's neck while Bradshaw attempted to knock him unconscious. Walter fought desperately, but the two men overpowered him. They tied the T-shirt around the top prison bars and backed off to watch Walter dangle, fighting thin air until he blacked out. He awoke lying on the floor. A guard had cut him down seconds after he passed out. Moved to the hospital wing of the prison, Walter grappled with the question of how to stay alive. There had been three attempts on his life. He had been to dozens of prisons. How could he stay alive? His existence was so fragile.

Inside himself he held enough rage to obliterate a nation, but in prison he was helpless. He hoped for the long shot. Perhaps his appeals would come through. It had been two years. If he could get out, he might have a fighting chance. In a few hours that hope exploded. Bonnie arrived for her visit, crying. Walter's attorney had contacted her to explain that all the appeals had been lost. As the words came out of her mouth, she began to bellow. She looked at Walter to catch a glimpse of something she had seldomly seen before – a tear rolling down his cheek. When he could, he spoke. "I want you to know how much I love you. I'm sorry for the way I've treated you. All I can do is tell you to go on with your life. Do what you need to do."

"I love you too," she burst out. "There's still hope."

"Oh Bonnie, why didn't you leave me a long time ago?" he said. He rubbed his eyes and walked her to the fence of the visiting area. She hugged him tightly and then pulled herself back. As she walked away he tried to call out to her. It was a weak whisper.

He took a deep breath. She heard him. "Bonnie, whatever you decide to do, I'll be your friend."

Back in his hospital room Walter lay across the bed. Even his teary good-bye was not a completely unselfish act. He gave her up to preserve his sanity. She would have left him anyway, he figured. He made the move for self-preservation, speeding up the inevitable. He was *afraid* to hold on. He felt regret and loss. But it was *his* regret that *he* couldn't have her and *his* loss that motivated him. He ran his fingers through his hair. He wanted her, wanted to possess her, body and soul. Nothing had changed. He was as selfish as ever, always selfish when it came right down to it. He rolled over on his stomach, closed his eyes, and meditated on Bonnie, what he would do with her and what he would do to others if he ever got out.

It was too risky to have Walter stay at the same prison for long. He was transferred to the large Florida State Penitentiary and sent to the east unit. The east unit contained a well-publicized isolation wing, R-Wing, better known by its accurate nickname, Death Row. Prison officials were now convinced that Death Row was the only place they could keep him safe.

The Florida State Penitentiary was home to Florida's worst criminals. Death Row was home to the worst of the worst. Walter could not have landed in a more fitting place. Out of the 900 men in the penitentiary, only 300 were in population. The penitentiary housed many infamous men, among them Jack "Murf the Surf" Murphy, a master jewel thief, and Bob Erler, the "Catch-Me Killer." One cell over was John Spenkelink. Even Ricky Cavarro, the drug lord who had slaughtered Walter's friend in 1973, resided on Death Row.

Supervisor Lieutenant Moody tried to explain what life would be like there. "I've heard about you for a year now. Some big-leaguer's got $200,000 on your head. I knew you would end up here," he said. "This is the end of the line."

Walter was placed on Q-Wing, which was down and across from R-Wing. Q-Wing was for the "crazies," or those inmates who were emotionally unstable. Cameras monitored Q-Wing twenty-four hours a day, seven days a week. When the death penalty was restored in the state of Florida, the wing became a holding pen for men awaiting their execution. Walter could peer from his cell and see the leather, metal, and wood, of "Old Sparky" – the electric chair. Lieutenant Moody added one last bit of information before leaving. "Showers are on Monday, Wednesday, and Friday. If one toilet stops up, the whole floor will stop up. There's a lot to learn, but you'll get used to it."

The first inmate he met was Spenkelink. John Spenkelink, six-foot-one and gaunt, had black hair with one unusual streak of gray and a distinctive Boston accent. He was a tidy person, but his cleanliness had not landed him an apartment on Death Row. Walter had heard about Spenkelink before. He was the much publicized killer of a homosexual in a Tallahassee bar. The brutal slaying resulted in a life sentence and the death penalty if it were restored in the state of Florida. On the way to a special visiting park for Death Row inmates, Spenkelink and Walter conversed. After a few trips, Spenkelink raised his eyebrows and remarked, "I know a way out."

"There's no way out of this place for either one of us, pal," Walter responded.

"No, Walt, I mean a real way out. Have you ever heard about Jesus Christ?" Spenkelink asked.

"Has anyone ever told you you're a nut?" Walter shot back.

The exchanges continued. Walter taunted him. "All you've got is chain-gang religion. You know you're here for life so you've got religion to baby-sit you." The old Walter would have laughed at Spenkelink, but the new Walter detested him.

"No, Walt," Spenkelink would answer patiently. "What I've got is real. And whether I go to the chair or not, don't cry for me because I'm going to a better place. Make sure you go there, Walt."

"Well, don't worry about it," Walter said sarcastically. "There's no death penalty in Florida anyway, so just keep your Jesus to yourself."

Spenkelink's evangelical work was interrupted abruptly. In November of 1977, Walter was leaving the prison commissary with a cup of milk. He noticed a man waiting near the exit door. The man stood silent with his hands sunk into a winter jacket. Walter had received stares before. There were many homosexuals in prison, so he thought nothing of it and strolled by, milk in hand. As he passed the doorway the man swung around and jabbed a spoon into Walter's side with all his strength. The cup of milk hit the floor and splattered. The round edge of the spoon was not designed for such a maneuver. The thrust was worse than a knife wound could have ever been. The man struggled and pushed the wide, dull spoon until his hand smacked against Walter's flesh. Still unsatisfied, he ripped the spoon from left to right with both hands. Walter screamed out. Blood hit the floor and splattered. The pain was excruciating. The man ran and Walter slumped to the floor.

Doctors cringed when they saw the trench that had been dug in his stomach. They marveled. "A spoon! God, how awful." One hundred eighty-two stitches from left to right finally sealed the wound. Walter was not safe at the Florida State Penitentiary, not even in the high security of Death Row.

He was relocated to Lake Butler Reception Medical Center, where he spent time resting and healing. The ordeal had been terrifying. This fourth attempt on his life was a brutal example of what lay ahead. Transferred from prison to prison, death was always one step behind and closing in.

His demented fantasies continued. No longer thinking about Bonnie, his tortured mind centered on nameless, faceless victims. He wondered if the man who had stabbed him had received pleasure from the deed. Walter knew *he* would have. It had been a long time since he had held a gun in his hands. He longed for a gun and a woman, any woman would do, but the gun had to be loaded.

At odd moments, he thought about Spenkelink. He resented the homosexual-killer's crusade to "save his soul." It was wrong somehow, revolting, that a convicted murderer, a man who had taken a life in cold blood would talk to him about Jesus Christ. Had Spenkelink no shame? There was more. How could God call a murderer His own? Now *that* was sick. Walter believed in God and he would never try to insult Him by claiming to be anything other than a thief. Who did Spenkelink think he was? At least *he* wasn't a hypocrite. The most distressing aspect of the Spenkelink situation, however, was that the man had latched onto something. The idiot was so calm and collected, so peaceful, loving, giving, and patient. Walter couldn't get to him, couldn't provoke him or penetrate whatever it was he had. Walter was bitter while Spenkelink was peaceful. He accepted Walter's attacks with humility and responded to his hatred with kindness.

Walter could not brush off the Spenkelink phenomena. Spenkelink was a specter who loomed larger than life. Clearly something had happened to him. A lobotomy might explain the peace, Walter knew about those, but what about the dynamic love? The man was not a vegetable, not passive. Walter had never experienced such a power in his life. He recoiled from it. Denied it. Tried to ignore it. It was clear, though; Spenkelink was the yucca plant in the barren desert called Death Row. Unattractive in appearance, unexpected in location, but a source of life for desert-dwellers. Fellow inmates flocked to him. Walter refused to sample the nourishment. Something inside him fought against it. He was suspicious. Spenkelink had a super con going, but what was the man's angle? Where was the payoff? Spenkelink's message was tenacious. It continued to look for an entry, but when Walter left the Florida State Penitentiary, he was confident it had found none.

Years later, wh*en the death penalty was revived in Florida, Spenkelink was the first man to be electrocuted. He burned in the huge chair until he died. When Walter heard the news, he felt queasy, nauseous. Spenkelink was different.*

42

CHAPTER FORTY-TWO

The perversion was becoming a malignancy, with a life of its own, spreading and eating away at his sanity.

All day, every day, sitting alone, he schemed, concocting weird methods of revenge. His condition and suffering were no fault of his own, he reasoned. Rather, the causes lay outside himself. He never bothered to discover those causes or to analyze and define them. Terms such as *heredity, environment* and *society* did not fit into his thought patterns. He had a vague concept of society, the system, the establishment. These were all bad, the personification of the enemy, and these, all of them, however one defined them, were at the bottom of his woes. And throw in a few people, people who had been directly involved in bringing about his troubles, people who were themselves victims of the system, but no less guilty, and he had sufficient identification to wreak havoc. Once he wished to beat the system, show how much smarter he was than it. Now, he wanted to hurt it, wound it, destroy it, all of it and everything about it. His was a passionate desire for vengeance. He was deserted and alone, the four attempts on his life, sobering reminders that he wanted to live. The suicide had failed. People didn't seem to care much anyway, and if they wouldn't feel sorry for him or respect him, what right did they have to live? He was a Dinnertime Burglar. He was a hit man. He was an extortionist. Those were important accomplishments. People should have paid him his due. He deserved respect. Fools! Didn't they realize how skilled he was at his craft? They did not, evidenced by the fact that he sat in prison.

In October of 1975, just before going to prison, Walter told *Miami Herald* staff writer Robert Liss, "I'm one of the really big ones, my friend. Hollywood is going to do my life story." But in a later interview, his last, after he had been battered in several of his trials, the starch was crumbling. He said, "I've got to serve a long sentence now – I don't know how long and I've got no guarantees from anyone. I feel like a man without a country . . . It would be good," he continued, "to have a friend." But he had no friends. Not one. He remained friendless for the next two years. The product of such conditioning was a mindless craving to enjoy brutality and lasciviousness. He wanted to titillate his senses with every vice his wild imagination could devise.

In 1979, just four years after entering prison, he was given the opportunity to turn his sick visions into concrete realities. A new prison system was introduced by the Florida legislature. It was called the point system. First-time offenders who had served fifty-three months or more were given parole dates. Walter's parole was set for February 12, 1980. Six months prior to this date, in August, he was placed on a work release program in Jacksonville, Florida. Inmates on work release lived in a supervised house, but during the day and up to eleven at night they were free to work and socialize. The contract was still out on his life. At least outside of prison he had the opportunity to clear his name, perhaps prove that he had not "turned over." As usual, he decided to forgo such reasonable thinking. He was excited about making money and finding a woman: money, anyway he could get it, and the comforts of a female as soon as possible. These were the priorities. He found a woman, then he found a girlfriend. It was as simple as that. He needed security, a steady sexual diet to make up for five years, and he needed to have someone want him. After this priority had been met, he looked for money.

A Jacksonville businessman, Bill Cook, had a company called Kool-O-Matic and took on Walter as a salesman. Cook offered him $500 a week and a Lincoln Continental. "Why hire a guy out of prison?" Walter wondered.

The truth slowly emerged at a bar. Cook explained that he was having serious problems with two men who had invested in Kool-O-Matic Walter recalls. He wanted to terminate their careers permanently. "I'll need help, someone else to go on the payroll," Walter stressed.

"Fine," the portly Cook assured him.

"Hey, you must have heard about me or something, right?" Walter asked.

"Yeah, I've heard about you," Cook responded.

Walter returned to the work-release house swollen with pride. He placed a phone call to Pete Floyd. Pete, an old friend in Fort Lauderdale, agreed to be his driver. *(Donaldson was unavailable. In 1978 he was shot in the head three times and dumped in a field on the outskirts of Miami.)*

After the conversation with Cook, it really began to feel good to be free. No doubt about it, he was great, as great as they come. *A killer. The guy knows I'm a killer.* He couldn't wait to select the gun. *This will be my best one yet,* he promised himself. He marveled that the world was able to keep itself occupied without him. *It must have been a boring four years.*

Several days later he was waiting in his girlfriend's

apartment when she rushed through the door screaming, "I will not love a murderer."

"What?" he shot back. She had been shaken down by the FDCLE. They warned her about Walter's past, adding that they had heard him, through a voice gun, discussing a murder contract. The FDCLE did not give Walter time to make up with his girlfriend. His work release was revoked and in a matter of hours he was sitting in Lawtey Correctional Institute. His head was on fire. He was on the verge of hitting it big again, and the system had stopped him in his tracks. It was rotten. He had had a taste, but it had been jerked away before he could swallow. At least he knew he was respected out there.

He was no two-bit crook. People knew. Lawtey was a temporary setback, not a defeat. He could win. The system had gotten the best of him in the past with numbers and raw power. What the system did not have was cunning, smarts. The system was dumb, hypocritical. It professed to uphold law, to defend justice. It really believed in neither and therefore it was uncertain and weak. Walter knew what he wanted. The system fired a shotgun a thousand feet away and showered down harmless pellets that stung a bit. But he knew how to fire a pistol up close. He knew how to hit the bull's-eye. Yes, he would beat the system. The system always hesitated before responding. That brief hesitation, that split second of indecision, that was his advantage. This time, after Lawtey, he would be finished with prisons forever. In the meantime he would bide his time. He would be a "good boy," the epitome of rehabilitation. The "dumb bastards" running the system, the superintendents, the case workers, the psychologists and chaplains, fed on rehabilitation. They needed "changed men" to justify their salaries and to secure bigger appropriations. Yes, he would be a star pupil, a rehabilitated "wonder of the world," and they would push for his release as a trophy of their success.

On February 12, 1980, just as he had predicted, he made parole and was a free man. While at Lawtey he had met Frank "The Wop" Gaglardi, an old-time mobster who had earned a lot of residual respect in organized crime. Walter convinced The Wop that he had never ratted on anyone, and The Wop, holding tight to a strict code of Mafia justice, decided that Walter should be cleared. He instructed Walter to look up an associate on the outside who would assist in getting the contract canceled. Finding Gaglardi's contact was easy enough, but futile. The contact and his associates were in hot water themselves. Getting them to make an appeal for him was like asking Benedict Arnold to defend a man charged with espionage. Walter would have to shelve his appeal to another day. More pressing matters needed attention. At the top of the list was improving his life-style.

Pete Floyd had given him an open invitation to join him in burglarizing. With a few calls Walter located Dale McClain and Marshall Perlow, both of whom were out on parole. They hugged each other like lost brothers. After their separation, it was still like old times. The four-man team went to work. Their home base was in Jacksonville, but raids took them south to familiar territory. The first night's work yielded $65,000 after the fence. Palm Beach residents, who for several years now had thrown accolades at law enforcement officials for keeping their community safe and peaceful, suddenly felt that they were in a war zone. Hunting season was open again. They were fair game. Walter possessed an unparalleled enthusiasm for his work. His plans for revenge were suffocated in the pure pleasure of burglary. For the time being, he was having too much fun to hate. Perlow, McClain, and Floyd heaped compliments on him. "Old Walt's the best there's ever been!"

His name had been plastered across every south Florida newspaper. He was the Dinnertime Burglar. Each alarm he disconnected and every jewel he collected met with a round of applause in his mind. In the past, he was earning a living. Now he was showcasing. He believed somehow that people knew it was he after discovering their valuables missing. "Look, Mom, that daring, debonair jewel thief Walter Shaw has craftily made off with our jewels again" – "I know honey, what can we do to stop him, he's the best." He was convinced that people admired him because he was uniquely deserving of admiration. The newspapers had solidified his fame. They reported the touching story of an elderly woman in a wheelchair with a bowel condition who, upon finding Walter midway through cleaning out her jewels, requested that he take her to the restroom. Walter obliged, wheeled her into the bathroom, helped her situate herself on the john, and then left. She commented that he was a gentleman bandit. *Any homeowner could respect that*, he assured himself.

Respectable Walter Shaw bought himself a new gray Continental from part of the proceeds lifted from the elderly woman he had placed on the toilet. It was the most expensive ride she had ever taken, and she had made several trips around the world.

Though superficially things seemed to be fine, down deep somewhere in the recesses of Walter mind there lay an exposed nerve. Caught up in his new-found success, basking in the profuse compliments of his crew, and cruising down expressways, sucking in the aroma of the leather-upholstered Continental, most of the time he maneuvered around the nerve. But then, in unexpected moments, he touched it, and when he did, he wanted to scream out. He had caught "the sickness unto death" after his break with The Bear. This had spawned the realization that there was no pinnacle on which to perch. Life was lived on an even grade with no meaning. The suicide attempt had been a response to that realization but not an answer. Just weeks after his parole, in the midst of cash and egogratification, that exposed nerve began to send steady, painful signals to his brain again. At first they were faint, yet consistent, reminders that contentment would not be his.

One night after a party he returned to Jacksonville's Thunderbird Motel. Dale McClain was enjoying a nineteen-year-old prostitute named Rose. Tired, Walter handed the girl $200 and told her to go home. As she opened the door to leave, she promised to introduce Walter to a friend of hers named Marianne.

Marianne was a redhead. She was voluptuous. No timid princess, her raw beauty had been displayed in the centerfold of a best-selling porn magazine. The pleasure of her company for a few hours was purchased at the astronomical price of $1,500, a figure comparable to the fee paid highfashion models to walk down runways. Walter met her and fell desperately in love. He had to have her, not for a night, but permanently. It happened suddenly. All questions were unequivocally answered by his instincts. She was gorgeous. What he felt may not have been love, but that didn't matter.

Bonnie had served him divorce papers shortly before he had left prison in 1977. It was not unexpected, but the finality of the act and receiving the papers in prison when he was so helpless had almost destroyed him. There had always been Bonnie. Until prison he had not lived alone, had not slept by himself, since he was a teenager. He did not court Marianne. He lunged for her, a frantic, desperate lunge.

They started living together and after a few days decided to get married. Marianne insisted on being married by a preacher. A prostitute since fifteen, a church wedding was her one claim to legitimacy. An attempt at the First Baptist Church of Jacksonville, Florida, met with resistance. Its pastor, Dr. Homer Lindsay, Jr., asked them if they were born again. Walter laughed. He hadn't heard the term "born again" since Spenkelink. "No, friend, we were born once, just like you." Dr. Lindsay could not join them in matrimony since they were not Christians. Walter cursed his way out of the sanctuary, angered at what he considered to be a put down by this overweight minister. Next, he contacted Larry Boardman, former middleweight boxing champion of the world. The Jewish boxer had quit the ring after a conversion to Christianity.

Boardman offered a solution. He knew a pastor who would marry them on the condition that they attend his church. Marianne was ecstatic. One church service to sanctify their vows would be a breeze. She called her two daughters to tell them the news. The Sunday-night church service started at 7:00.

43

CHAPTER FORTY-THREE

"Are you ready, honey?" Walter called out.

"Almost," came a giggle. Then several more. A pale white smoke, the unmistakable aroma of marijuana, seeped from under the bathroom door. Marianne and her two daughters, thirteen and fifteen, were preparing themselves for church. This Rastafarian ritual held no religious significance for them. They merely wished to be high, not holy. The door opened and the three charged out. "It's going to be fun," Marianne laughed.

Larry met the foursome on Druid Street at the First United Pentecostal Church. Walter was nervous. He wanted to throw up, while his fianceé and future stepdaughters could not have been more enthusiastic. Thoughts of prison popped into his mind. Never did he imagine that he would be free, driving to a pentecostal church with a call girl – centerfold model and her two children, all of whom were stoned, to expedite a marriage ceremony.

He saw a junkyard. The church, sitting next to a junkyard, was a big step down from the colossal downtown Baptist church. It was a rundown wooden building, the faded white paint peeling off. Opening the car door, he cocked his head to hear the beat of drums, the blast of horns, and the rattle of tambourines. "What's the music?" Walter asked.

Larry looked to the church. "It's the service."

"No way," Walter blurted out.

Larry Boardman laughed. Marianne laughed. Her two daughters laughed. Everyone laughed except Walter. He trembled. When Larry opened the front door to the delapidated old building, the blasting music pounded his ears. He nearly tripped and fell. It was like a club on Miami Beach. He had walked right into Mardi Gras. The entire congregation stood with hands stretched toward the ceiling. "Larry, shit, these people are being robbed," he exclaimed.

Larry, a little agitated, hushed him. "Please, Walt, they're worshipping the Lord."

"That's how they worship?" Walter quizzed him, like a child. Then his worst nightmare came true. Larry ushered them down the long isle to the *front row*. It took forever. On all sides he was surrounded by jumping, jerking, jubilant maniacs. He was being led through a freak show or an asylum, except unfortunately there were no bars to separate him from the crazies. Walter cringed as Marianne and her daughters, feeling the beat, almost danced to the front, laughing with each step. Walter held the somber gaze of a pallbearer at a funeral.

Though Marianne was high and growing more obnoxious, it was his solemn presence that stuck out in the crowd. He was on the verge of panic. One elderly woman started dancing in the aisle, oblivious to aging limbs ordinarily incapable of such energetic gyrations. Walter was preparing to run out. Larry, sensing his mood, ordered "stay," pointing his finger firmly as if talking to an unruly dog.

"They're jamming," Walter finally managed.

Marianne, clapping with the congregation, turned and

whispered in a shattering screech. "They're holy rollers. Holy rock-and-rollers!" She and her daughters flashed red-slitted eyes at their neighbors in the other pews. The churchgoers smiled back. Every few minutes something horrible would happen to someone in the congregation. Shouts of "Sweet Jesus," "Halleluja" and "Praise the Lord" burst through the music at full vocal capacity. Walter jerked in sheer horror at each outburst. He had recently read an article about Jim Jones and the Guyana tragedy. He thought about Jim Jones until he could contain himself no longer. "Are they going to hurt us?" he asked Marianne desperately. She didn't hear him. *What am I doing asking a stoned woman that question for?*

The beat kept coming. Suddenly, an athletic middle-aged man picked up a saxophone and began to belch out a tune.

"Where is the priest?" Walter asked Larry. Larry pointed toward the exuberant saxophone player. His name was Wil Cohron. Boardman later explained that he held a track record for the state of Florida. He was robust and attractive at forty-three. When he finished his song, perspiration glistened on his forehead and soaked through his shirt. He put down the saxophone and rushed to the pulpit. "God has changed my sermon. I had planned to speak on something else, but the Lord has laid another message on my heart. I take my text from the book of Ecclesiastes."

The message lasted over an hour. The laughter ceased long before its close. Marianne was sober. An unsettling warmth broke in to Walter's chest and spread across his body midway through the message. A thought crossed his mind. He began to boil. *Larry must have told him about me – this is a setup.* Pastor Cohron had delivered a message from one of the Bible's existentialist masterpieces. He spoke of life, its futility, meaninglessness and vanity. He described down to minute detail the disease that had afflicted Walter for years. He warned: This sickness is unto death. He expanded on the fragile state of life as if he knew about the four attempts that had been made to eliminate Walter. He examined life's hopelessness as if he had heard about Walter's near suicide. He exposed the vanity of life as if he had seen the mockery and superficiality of Walter's existence. He closed his message with two of literature's most famous passages, taken from Ecclesiastes. "Then shall the dust return to the earth as it was; and the spirit shall return unto God who gave it. Vanity of vanities, saith the preacher, all is vanity."

Walter had been confronted. He saw himself, recognized for a fleeting moment that he was the vainest of the vain. But the recognition only lasted a split second. Another matter, much closer, and in his mind more urgent, required attention. Marianne was crying. Her mascara had turned into a sticky black slop and formed a muddy river streaming down her cheeks. She was unaware of her appearance, and the tears flowed faster and faster. She sobbed. "Can't you see? It's all a waste of time."

He turned away, but Larry caught his eye. "Would you like to go down?" he asked.

"Leave me alone!" Walter hissed angrily. Marianne rushed to the wooden altar beneath the pulpit. A dozen women surrounded her and began to cry with her and touch her. Their beehive hairdos shook with urgency. Marianne cried uncontrollably and moved erratically. She was loud, everyone heard her. Perspiration beaded Walter's forehead. If he stayed he would blow. The pastor kept watching him. Larry stared too. The tension was unbearable. The praying and shouting were unbearable. The crying was unbearable. The feeling that everyone was looking at him and that he had done something wrong was unbearable. Finally, he broke from the mysterious hold, pushed out the church doors, and felt the cool night air slap his face and curl around his head. The noise died. He walked to the car, leaned against it, and waited.

Maybe twenty minutes later, he wasn't certain, Larry cracked the church door open and motioned for Walter. "I'm staying out here where it's safe, you freak!" he said arrogantly. At that moment he remembered Spenkelink. He remembered his revulsion. Both Spenkelink and the preacher here tried to bring him down. Why should they interfere, he never harassed them. "Your fianceé is going to get baptized," Larry shouted.

Someone had to stop this madness.

Marianne rushed to him. "I want to get baptized, Walt."

He walked back inside. "What are you asking me for? It's your life? Don't ask me for permission to do this crap," he almost shouted. The crazy crowd needed to hear his disdain. The beehives took her arms and led her back to the front. Walter called down the aisle, "I thought you wanted to get married?"

Minutes later the music resumed and the pastor's brother, Metric Cohron, walked into a narrow baptismal pool with black waist-high rubber waders. He looked like a dazed fisherman. Walter watched as Marianne followed Metric Cohron into the water.

"I baptize you in the name of the Father,

In the name of the Son,

And in the name of the Holy Ghost."

He pushed her under. A small splash. She came up shouting, illuminated and more beautiful than ever. There was a radiance about her face. Walter listened closely, something in her voice was captivating. She sounded free. That was enough. He started to back up and stumbled into Larry. "What's wrong?" Larry asked.

"Never mind," he whispered as he left the building.

People began to leave the church. Walter, standing by the car, watched for Marianne. She did not come out. When the lights went out in the sanctuary, she emerged with her two daughters, Larry and Pastor Cohron. As they headed to the car, Walter interrupted the conversation. "What happened to you?" he asked.

She flashed a strong smile, "Oh, Walt, when I went under I asked God to forgive me and he did." Walter did not comment. He was safely concealed in a shadow, no one could see his face. He closed his eyes.

"God doesn't want us to get married until you get saved," she continued.

"What? What in the hell are you talking about, Marianne? You came here tonight to marry me," he protested.

"I can't marry you, son. You two would be unequally yoked. Now that she is a believer, I can't join you in matrimony," the pastor responded.

"Is he for real?" Walter asked Larry.

"Walt, he can't . . . ," Larry began.

"Just shut up! Everybody shut up!" Walter interrupted. "If you ain't for real, Mr. Preacher, you're gonna meet God sooner than you ever thought possible." Marianne started to apologize to Pastor Cohron, but Walter ordered her in the car. "Remember what I said, preacher," Walter warned before getting in himself. "This better be real and it better not be one of those Jim Jones deals."

The next few weeks Walter undertook the massive task of deprogramming Marianne. She had caught something, that was for sure. Repeatedly she said that she loved him, loved him even more, in a deeper way. The Lord was teaching her to love now, she said. But as much as she wanted to marry him, she could not. She wanted a Christian home, wanted to serve the Lord with a husband who loved God. He could not give her that. He threatened to walk away and never come back. She cried and begged him not to leave. He burst out with sarcasm toward her, toward the crazies at the church, and he hurled filthy remarks about Pastor Cohron at her. Every conversation started softly, rationally, and ended with her crying and him shouting obscenities. But he refused to relent. He wanted her. He had to have her, God and all. He pounded away, and finally she succumbed.

Once they married, she convinced herself, she could persuade him to become a Christian. Walter's plans moved in another direction. When he fell in love with her, he believed she would be the perfect wife, a good-time girl who would not gripe or complain about his burglaries and late-night engagements. Marianne was fun. Whatever spell the church had put on her would wear off in time. This "Praise the Lord" stuff was beneath money and good times. He would bury it.

44

CHAPTER FORTY-FOUR

They were married by a notary public. Walter promised to make up for it. He bought diamonds, cars, furs, and even a dog as consolation. She, in turn, sold the jewels, the cars, the furs, and the dog, handing the proceeds over to the church. Walter was too busy stealing to stop her. She liquidated every asset he collected with missionary zeal. If he continued his burglaries, the profits might as well go to a good cause, she decided. To make matters worse, when she wasn't selling his goods, she was in church. She attended the two, three, and sometimes four-hour services five or six nights a week. "Damn it, if I haven't married a John Spenkelink," he cursed. "Maybe God will give us a little time together one day, honey," he would jeer as she left the house with her new Bible.

When without so much as telling him, she sold a piece of property he had purchased as an investment, he decided to take action. She was not the problem. The entire fiasco traced its roots back to that Jimmy Swaggart-looking fruitcake of a pastor. Walter stormed into Cohron's office, slammed his fist on the desk, and demanded a refund. The pastor responded, kindly but unafraid. "I can't return the money, Walt; it belongs to the Lord."

"Oh really, has God been breaking into houses lately? . . . Listen, keep the money, but just tell God to leave me alone."

Back at home the arguments were more frequent and intense. Walter called Pastor Cohron at least once a week just to make sure he remembered his opinion of him. He became more belligerent. The more Walter pounded her, the more determined Marianne seemed. The days drifted into months. Finally, his cruelty reached a level beyond her tolerance. One night, in the heat of an argument, she ran from the house, unsure of where to go and unsure of her marriage. At last her newfound faith had been shaken, and, at last, he had won. He had gotten to her, and she would return, he thought. She did not.

Walter sat around the empty apartment for days. One of the reasons he had been creating such a ruckus was to avoid thinking. The words of the pastor troubled him; they came to him over and over again. He rebelled against them, struggled not to give in. He was fully aware of the consequences of a ceasefire. It would signify that he was wrong, not just to burglarize or brutalize, but wrong from the beginning. His first meditated acts of violence would then be considered error. His conclusion that his father had been victimized would require alteration. And all the logic that said that he had been betrayed or forced into his life-style would be invalid.

Sitting in the apartment he raced through his youth. *The New York Times* report would be correct. His dad *would* be a mobster. There *would* be a difference between Uncle Archie and law-abiding citizens. *Uncle Archie would be wrong.* The last twenty-five years of his life would have been based on a lie. His suicide would not have been a *reaction* but a controlled *action*. To accept Pastor Cohron's thesis would cause breakdown, apocalypse. It would ultimately mean that he could be held responsible for every action he had taken in his life. He would be to blame – all of Bonnie's woes, his children's unhappiness his fault. His depression and emptiness a product of his own design. That would make him one of the cruelest bastards and shallowest idiots on the face of the planet. He would be a first-rate clown. No, he could never accept that.

    He tried to shake off the inner turmoil by driving to south Florida. The familiar landscape and seeing his good-time friends would alleviate the turmoil. Instead, his anxiety increased. He began to foul up his jobs. He lacked concentration. Things became dangerous, and his gang began to doubt his competence. The situation was disastrous. It would be only a matter of time until he made one mistake too many. Late one night after a score he called pastor Cohron. He was inebriated, hurling insults over the phone. "Say, preacher, why do you keep talking to me, anyway? Do you get off on talking to a big-league criminal?" Walter slurred.

    "No, Walter, as a person I don't like you and wouldn't want to have anything to do with you, but the Christ in me loves you, I'm obedient," Cohron responded.

    A few seconds of silence passed as the words shot through Walter's buzzing head. "Well, I think you're a nut." He hung up.

    Unable to effectively steal, he returned to Jacksonville and moved in with Larry Boardman. Why violate his parole by being out of Jacksonville, since he wasn't going to profit from it? The days were excruciatingly long. The nights were worse. He was unable to return to his old frame of mind. The truth was unavoidable. He resolved to lie about it for the rest of his life. Then he realized that such deception would be impossible. Refusing to think about the past or the future, he was painfully aware of the present. The discomfort was more than misery or depression, it was an asphyxiating state of limbo. *Vanity of vanities of vanities of vanities of vanities.* He could not escape the message. It awakened him at night and blinded him by day. It filled his belly with knots. He could not eat. It flooded his mind with confusion. He could not find peace. He had fleeting thoughts of admitting to his mistakes but stopping there. "Okay, I'm guilty, so what?" Terror closed in. Private admissions did not exorcise it. He only pushed himself further down a path which, he was slowly learning, offered no return.

Since his disillusionment with The Bear he had been bounding down this hated path, although he did not recognize it earlier. Each step brought him to a deeper, more conscious understanding of where he had been and who he was. The facts were unpleasant. The sickness locked on more tightly, wrenched out all self-deception, exposed secret after secret, until he was flaming with self-consciousness. *This sickness was unto death.* He knew it was. And finally the self-consciousness, the revelation of who and what he was and what he had done brought him, at long last, to self-condemnation.

A week before Thanksgiving of 1980, he went for a drive. He drove up and down street after street, fast and slow. He passed a bar, thought about going inside, but drove on. He re-thought his way through his life, not event after event, but generally, the big panoramic view. Every conclusion was re-examined. Guilty – not guilty? Responsible? Was the present anguish, so relentless and draining, a phase, or was it permanent? An onslaught of questions overpowered him. Then the vivid dark visions faded. His mind shifted into dull half-speed. Something had snapped. Right there in his Cadillac, something snapped. Had he given up? He did not know. Everything went dull. He passed another bar, slowed down, then sped away. He circled the block, stopped roadside and rested. Minutes later he restarted the car. The roads, winding and straight, that tracked throughout Jacksonville seemed clogged. He could not simply choose a road and continue driving. Every road, except one, appeared endless and uninviting. He did not want to drive forever. One road held a destination. All the other avenues seemed circular while this road dead-ended. It frightened him to come to the end of the road, but it was unavoidable.

With increasing speed he headed toward what he saw as the lesser of two evils, the deadend, the destination – Druid Street. He arrived at 9:30, several hours late for a Thursday-night service. The crazies were already up front praying. He walked straight down, veered off to the side, and knelt at the corner of the altar. No one came to greet him. He reached into his blue-and-white jacket and pulled out a prized and favorite possession, one of his old Browning .9 millimeters. After laying it on the altar, someone began playing the organ. It was beautiful. A tear dropped in front of him. Walter looked up. Pastor Cohron stood next to him crying. The preacher knelt and curled an arm around his head. Walter broke down. His heart tore open, ripped wide, and he cried unashamedly – not out of sadness, depression, futility, or frustration, certainly not out of joy. He wept because he was guilty, because – and it came in a flash – he was responsible, responsible for every problem, for every theft, for the divorce, for leaving his children, for so many hurt and broken people he could not remember all of them. Yes, he was responsible, personally and directly responsible – not his father, not The Bear, not the system, but he, himself, had heaped upon himself all the bad that had come his way. "I am shit," he mumbled.

His whole body shook. Tears flooded his eyes. He could not control them. He did not want to control them. Then, unexpectedly, he sensed an unfathomable presence and was consumed in awe. Something pure, in which he could find no fault, surrounded him and moved through him. Later, he marveled that a man who had entered a church door only a handful of times and had never read a Bible could have had such a striking, clear, and unmistakable confrontation with Jesus Christ. But there Christ was, just as Spenkelink had said he would be.

"Pray with me, Walt," Cohron urged. Walter listened and repeated: "Lord, you know who I am. I've stolen all my life. You know what I've done. I am a sinner. But I know you'll forgive me, and I commit my life to you. It's just not working my way". The prayer was brief. As much as it was a finale, it was a beginning.

The sickness ended in death. Walter Shaw died that night. Later he read the words of the Apostle Paul : "Yet not I live but Christ lives in me." King James's English was difficult, but *that* he understood. Marianne's glow too! Forgiven! Unbelievable! It was as if he had jumped into an abyss, blindly hoping beyond hope, and instead of annihilation he found transformation, renewal, and *salvation.*

Pastor Cohron held him like a child. Walter cried on and on. The single burning impression was Christ. From a man who knew no sin, he, one of the chief sinners, became aware of love everlasting. He would never forget. He would never be the same.

Soon the other churchgoers huddled around him. He was hugged by people he had never seen. Laughter, warmth, handshakes, forgiveness. It was an amazing, life-changing grace that accepted him. He smiled as the organ played, his mind bathed in a sweet peace, his heart beating fresh, he basked in the magnificent sway of forgiveness.

While it was true that he had been responsible for each destructive incident in his past, he knew it was also true that he had been forgiven for his past – all of it. He could not explain it, nor did he need to do so. A presence, more intimate and loving than any he had known, enveloped him. It stifled all doubts, wasted every fear, decimated his insecurities, flooded his guilt with wholeness, and submerged his hatred in love.

This was it. Finally he had found it. Searching, as he had been all his life, for strength and profound power, he recognized this presence as that for which he had been so fervently seeking. Uncle Archie failed, Sacco failed, Tom Palmer failed, Salerno failed, The Bear failed, and at last he had failed. *Is there no one who has real power, is there no one who does not fail?* This question had been answered.

Two words that to Walter Shaw had always been antonyms, love and power, united in his mind. Love was not weakness, and what he viewed as power was not strength. He determined that anything which could make his life worth living, anything that could change him was power. Here it was. The antonyms became synonyms. Love was real power, lasting power, life-changing power. Finally, he had found it, confronted it, indeed, hit it head on. The most real and powerful thing in the universe – the love of God.

45

CHAPTER FORTY-FIVE

The First United Pentecostal Church of Jacksonville, Florida, did not practice delayed gratification. At eleven P.M. that same Thursday night, Walter was baptized, and Pastor Cohron kept him into the morning hours teaching him. Walter may have changed, but his past had not. Cohron knew this. God may have forgiven him, but the rest of His creation would not accept his newfound faith as readily. Will Cohron patiently explained this state of affairs. Walter was so intoxicated with the new freedom he had received that he had difficulty believing anything could ever go wrong again.

For the first time since he was a teenager he went out looking for a job. Openings were limited for an ex-con experienced in burglary, whose only references came from the underworld. He was hired as a construction worker at the Woodbine Naval Station in Woodbine, Georgia, at four dollars per hour. A step down in pay from $40,000 an hour, give or take a few thousand, to four dollars an hour, necessitated a harsh change in his life-style. Once established, he placed several important phone calls to his old gang. He told them that he would not be coming back to work. A couple of them laughed at him, saying, "We'll be right here when it passes, Walter." One angrily hung up on him. Several friends even had the audacity to congratulate him for conceiving a new and convincing con. Most simply did not believe him. The few who did hated him. He never expected such resistance.

Pastor Cohron bought him a pocket New Testament and Walter devoured it, reading every line again and again. Every day for two hours he met with the pastor and discussed what he had read and what he felt. Initially the radical transformation made him euphoric. He believed that his conversion experience had left him free *from* all evil. He grew frustrated and even afraid when the belief was tested and proved to be untrue.

Some of his fellow workers belittled and harassed him. He reminded himself of his new command – "Love thy neighbor as thyself" – but his anger swelled up all the same. Sometimes he even pondered permanently silencing his antagonistic co-workers. He would leave work disgusted with himself. Slowly he realized that serving Christ did not give him freedom *from* evil, it gave him power *over* evil. Christ himself, as Pastor Cohron expounded, was tempted in every way. In following Christ, Walter learned, one faces the heavy tow of temptation, but contrary to before, one can win over negative urges. Walter experienced an inward struggle. It was as if there were two of him – the new Walter and the old. To his horror, often there was more old in him than new.

His inability to always behave as he supposed a Christian should tormented him. He explained this sensation to Pastor Cohron, wondering if perhaps he had been only "halfway" accepted by God. "No," the pastor assured him, turning through his Bible and quoting from the Apostle Paul. Walter read along as Cohron explained. Paul, the great builder of the Christian faith, cried out in frustration that the things that he knew he should do, he did not do, and the very things that he knew he should not do, he did. Paul talked about a war that raged in his body between the new and old selves. He even spoke of himself as "chief of sinners." Paul sinned. Paul grieved God after his conversion on the road to Damascus. Paul fell into temptation. Only Christ never sinned. That is why only Christ has the power to overcome sin. "Christ is everything," Walter concluded.

Walter had never been aesthetically inclined, but in Christ he found a source for his own artistic vision. He saw beauty in Christ, in himself, and in the world around him. Walter read about something called the "renewing of your minds." "Is that salvation?" he asked Pastor Cohron. He was comforted to learn that mind renewal begins with salvation, but is distinct from it. Mind renewal is the long-range process of becoming what God had originally intended mankind to be. Salvation is two-fold: Christ's birth into a life, and the creation of a new life, a new spirit, by Christ. Walter could hardly understand at first. However, from the beginning he *felt* it. Christ, distinct from him, was forcefully in his heart. And a new person, a better self, now occupied his body. In him also was his old nature. These were existential truths he could not verbalize.

Walter also realized that being a Christian was a daily decision to follow Christ. Some days, Walter learned, it was harder to make the decision than others. Often he was confronted by nagging doubts. He wondered if he hadn't actually "conned" himself. These moments came no more often, nor were they any more intense, than beautiful experiences with Christ. He felt like a yo-yo, up one minute and down the next. Evidently he would need to believe in the reality of his faith in spite of his emotions. Such a pattern of life was entirely foreign to Walter. He was the reigning prince of emotionalism. He had never, in all his life, acted out of reason, willpower, or belief. The gangsters he admired so much behaved the same way. Some of them were more sophisticated than he, but still, their lives swayed back and forth according to the winds of the day. Walter looked around him at church and found people deserving of genuine admiration. They were not powerful, wealthy or famous, but they held doggedly to their convictions, loved when most would hate, and waded through the morass that life often became, with vigor, resolution, and joy. They were heroes. Simple people with a common bond: They were all in love with Jesus Christ.

There were still deep pains. His new life was one of reconciliation, and there was none more urgent than his to Marianne. He had wounded her, ruined their love, and perhaps torn down her faith. To his surprise she forgave him, celebrated with him in his triumph, and on the tenth of December, they moved into the apartment together as husband and wife.

Immediately after reconciliation he noticed a significant change in Marianne, a negative one, which he was afraid to probe or investigate. Given his past behavior, he kept quiet. Unfortunately, his patience could not soothe her scared psyche. Day after day she grew more irritable and abrasive. Unexpectedly she quit going to church. Walter was stunned. He pleaded. That only pushed her further away. He realized that the tables had been turned. *But that's not it*, he rationalized. *I really love her – I don't mind revenge – just as long as she's Okay I just hurt because she's hurting.* He refused to accept the fact that he was receiving his due. Slowly he realized that he did not deserve to be self-righteous. He became humble.

He wept and prayed. Secretly, though he would not admit it, his faith was beginning to totter. Would he fall back into his old ways? Was the salvation experience only good for a month? As he watched his wife unravel, fear gripped him. The further away from Christ she went, the less she seemed to love him. Then, just two weeks after Walter's commitment to follow Christ, she started hitting highclass bars again, selling her favors. One night she told Walter that she was leaving to take care of a client. "You've probably seen the movie about him," she taunted. "Paul Newman played him; he's called 'Cool-Hand Luke'."

"What about us? You're my wife. And what about Christ? What's going on?" he yelled.

She walked toward the door. He couldn't allow her to leave, to sleep with a man for money, to lie with a man, to please, to satisfy, to enjoy a man. The situation was beyond his comprehension. The scene he was living out was straight from his past. It was all wrong. "You can't do this," he cried out, running in front of her to lock the door. "I won't let you go."

Perspiration dripped from his face. His body was bathed in it. Both of them began to scream. He yelled at her. "Why do I have to yell? Why is this happening?" He begged and threatened.

She turned to the kitchen and he followed. He reached out to grab her shoulder, but she jerked free and pulled a counter drawer open. Forks, spoons, and knives crashed to the floor.

"Honey, let's talk," he said, moving forward to take her into his arms.

She turned to face him. In the same second her arm thrust forward. He looked down – it seemed like slow motion and watching the flash of a stainless-steel paring knife rip through his blue sweatshirt and into his abdomen. He slumped to the floor. Blood seeped from his belly. Without the slightest bit of concern for him, she walked out of the kitchen, unlocked the front door, and slammed it behind her. He held the sweatshirt against the open wound and crawled to a phone. "Larry, man, she stabbed me right in my gut."

"I'll be right there," Larry promised.

"Larry?" Walter called out over the phone. His friend waited. Delirious and sinking, he sobbed out, broken to the core, "She's going to screw some guy. Please stop her. She's gonna screw him, Larry."

Larry arrived and rushed him to the hospital. The wound required twenty-seven stitches. Marianne returned several days later to announce, "I'm moving out. I came to get my stuff."

Walter sat quietly while she packed. As she made the last trip to the car, he sprang from the couch, "Wait, please" He began to cry. "I love you. I do, please stay."

The car door slammed. He grabbed the door handle. It was locked. Marianne put the car into reverse, backed out of the driveway, and screamed through the closed window, "Let go."

She hit the gas pedal hard and his body jerked several feet forward before he crashed to the pavement. He lay in the driveway, face down, calling her name. His shoulder tingled and ached when he raised himself up. Movement caused extreme pain. Larry took him to the hospital for the second time in three days. Xrays showed that his collarbone was broken. He spent the night with Larry. Christ had weakened him, he determined, stripped away his defenses and rendered him helpless. How could he protect himself? It seemed unfair that he had, by being a Christian, adopted a set of rules that no one else bothered to follow. How could he survive? He had lost his edge.

When Larry dropped him by his apartment, Marianne had returned. She met him at the door, put her arms around him and kissed him deeply. "I'm sorry," she said. Undoubtedly, he assumed, her appearance was an answer to prayer. Perhaps he was not so vulnerable after all.

The next morning, he took Marianne to pick out a

-240-

Christmas tree. (*Amazing! Things are turning around. The first good Christmas in years.*) On the way back to the apartment they stopped by the parole office for him to fill out his written report. He was greeted with handcuffs. Having been photographed in south Florida, officers had proof certain that he had violated the conditions of his parole. He called Pastor Cohron. "I've given my life to God and gone straight. Now look what happens!"

Pastor Cohron promised to help him. He went on to explain that Christianity was not an escape from responsibility, rather an acceptance *of* responsibility. He stated flatly, "Walter, what you sow is what you reap."

If that were the case, then Walter had a considerable amount of reaping to do and none of it pleasant. Through sheer force of habit he grew bitter. He prayed as best he could, trying to explain his frustration to God. The communication was effective. He began to understand. God had forgiven him and accepted him. But he had sinned against society too. He had to pay his debt. He accepted the burden of his wrongs without any anger toward God or prison officials. He could not be optimistic, however. First Marianne, now prison.

46

CHAPTER FORTY-SIX

Walter was shipped to Butner Federal Penitentiary in Durham, North Carolina. There he underwent psychological evaluations to determine if he was a recidivist. The results were negative. It was at Butner that he met a chaplain, Mrs. Cynthia Hale. She gave him several books, a New Testament, various study aids, and encouragement. When possible, he called Pastor Cohron. Despite ten to twelve hours of daily Bible reading and telephone calls to Pastor Cohron, he was rushing downhill. Then Marianne served him divorce papers. He went out of control. He wanted to destroy again.

Marianne had told him that his eyes were his most appealing feature. *Fine,* he thought, *I'll destroy my eyes.* He took a plastic container of Tinactin, a preparation for athletes foot, and studied it. The label clearly warned: "May cause blindness." With that, he cocked his head back and filled his eyes with the liquid, screaming as guards rushed him to the infirmary. He was blind. The doctor could not even promise that his vision would return. In the dark Walter vacillated from self-pity to self-chastisement. He had pulled another Shaw showstopper. Marianne, hearing about his latest stunt, was not impressed. She pushed the divorce through. The penitentiary psychiatrist diagnosed him as a manic-depressive. Pastor Cohron listened patiently to his long, melancholy discourses, which often erupted into bitter splots of vitriolic. "Where was God, huh? Why did he let this happen? Does he want me to be blind for the rest of my life?"

In the midst of these outbursts there was an acknowledgment, an understanding, one which he could not really verbalize or share with Pastor Cohron. He did not know how to express it, and even if he had had the words, he was still too steeped in pride to open up. For the first time, for the very first time in his life he knew, really knew, intellectually at least, that he was responsible. That night at church when he had placed his revolver on the altar and prayed with Pastor Cohron, he had, in that enormously electrifying experience, seen himself, and had emotionally accepted his guilt. But now, he *understood*. He not only knew that he was responsible for his life, but why he was responsible.

Walter knelt in his cell and asked for God's forgiveness again. He was incapable of ridding himself of himself. If God did not come to his rescue, did not somehow intervene, he would never live a sound and normal life. If indeed he had to pay, one by one, all the debts he owed, he would not be free and clear, even in a thousand years. He understood. He personally deserved what was coming his way, and the only hope he had of being sustained was the sheer grace of God. He confessed it all to God. One month later, his sight was restored.

From Butner he went to Lake Butler Medical Reception Center and stood before a parole board along with Pastor Cohron, who stated that he would take personal responsibility for Walter upon his release. The board granted Walter another parole in August 1981, and he went back to the Woodbine

Naval Station as a carpenter's helper. At night he put in time at the Eighth Street Detention Center in Jacksonville as a volunteer. There were no fancy nightclubs, drinking, or women. Yet a new life-or-death urgency gripped him. The flow of traffic in and out of the detention center was brisk. The person he spoke to one night would likely be gone the next. He passionately told young offenders about Christ. If Christ could turn him around, and He had, Christ could help anyone.

The nights were disappointing as well as rewarding. Walter confronted many of the ghosts of his past. Often, he was called a "nut," a "fruitcake," or worse. Some of the detainees simply refused to listen. "I'll work it out on my own" was a constant refrain. Still, Walter was effective. He was one of them. He knew. He was an insider, not a hypocritical do-gooder. When not at the detention center, he attended church. No longer did he flinch when church members jumped up or shouted "Praise the Lord." The hugging and handshaking, once terrifying, were now a source of tremendous pleasure. He marveled at himself. He was happy, fulfilled. The old life was light-years away. It was as if he had never been there.

47

CHAPTER FORTY-SEVEN

Near the end of September 1981, an old prison friend found Walter in Jacksonville. Richard Lee Ellwood was a loudmouth. Long, brown, stringy, hair hung in his eyes. Thin as a rail, five feet eight inches, 135 pounds, and just twenty-two, he had nearly been killed in prison for his cutting tongue. He possessed an uncanny knack for instigating chaos and hatred. As a fellow inmate Walter had tried to avoid him. Several inmates warned Ellwood that he better make it on the outside because if he ever came back to prison they would kill him.

Unintimidated by the threats, he proceeded to get himself caught red-handed in a robbery just a few weeks after his release from prison. He posted a $47,000 bond, putting up his mother's house as collateral. True to his nature, he then proceeded to jump bail, which guaranteed a foreclosure on his mother's home and eventually an extended prison term for himself. It was this latter possibility that motivated him to find Walter. He had to beat the prison rap. It wasn't the bars that disturbed him, but the people behind the bars. He begged Walter for help. "Do you know what they'll do to me?"

Walter did know. Ellwood would go down. To add more pitiable drama to his story Ellwood said, "If I don't make good on that bond, they'll take my mother's house, for God's sake, and then I go to jail. I have to come up with the money, Walt." Walter was moved. Ellwood was in trouble, and even though he was despicable, he was a human being.

Walter took the problem to Pastor Cohron. Cohron expressed sympathy, but $47,000 was far out of a country preacher's league. Walter asked Ellwood to allow him a few days to see if he could come up with some help.

Ellwood's timing could not have been worse. Walter had just enrolled in Luther Rice Seminary. Everything was going well. He was working, studying, and slowly putting together a new life. He tried to ignore Ellwood, pretending in his mind that he had never showed up and would not return. Ellwood not only returned, he also begged and pleaded. To Walter, Christ was love more than anything else. Christ was real, a lover of those who did not deserve love. Ellwood was no worse than he had been. In fact, Ellwood was a dumb twenty-two-year-old juvenile delinquent. He certainly did not deserve help, but he needed it. A prison term could be a death sentence. Ellwood had that figured right. Walter had only one way to help him, but Christ's love did not extend to a lapse back into burglary. *That is what Ellwood wanted.* Similar decisions would come along the rest of his life. He or someone would need money, and he would always be tempted to get it the easy way. Ellwood kept pleading. Either he produced the $47,000, and took his chances in court, or his mother would be thrown out of her house, and he would be thrown into jail.

Walter, for reasons he does not understand, set out on a course he had never tried before. He soaked himself in alcohol. In the past, through his worst problems, he had never resorted to booze. Now he drank regularly and heavily, and did his best to avoid Ellwood. The newly acquired habit alienated him from the Lord. He had turned to another source, and he felt disenfranchised, and questioned God's willingness to forgive him. At every turn Ellwood succeeded in tracking Walter down. Walter tried to be a friend, but their meetings were tense and combative.

On March 18, 1982, Walter was visiting Ellwood at his apartment when Detectives Mittleman and Carlson, as they later testified, arrived to arrest Ellwood for his bond-jumping and for several charges of robbing gas stations. The Appeal Brief of the Appellee (the State of Florida) records that "the purpose in going to the Alderman Road address was to arrest Ellwood on the outstanding warrants." When Walter heard the detective's knock on the door, he instinctively opened a front window and ran for his life. The brief continues on the testimony of Carlson and Mittleman – responding to an observer's "Yell that someone was coming out the window. Carlson turned and saw Appellant [Shaw] running east through the [apartment] complex. And at that time [Carlson] gave chase on foot and apprehended [Appellant] in the next building hiding underneath the stairwell." When detective Carlson cornered Shaw, his gun was already out. Shaw testified that "He pointed it at me and was going to kill me, but two small children wandered by. He told me that they must be my guardian angels because he was going to stop my burglarizing for good. He was going to blow my brains out."

If the children were an answer to a prayer, that prayer would have belonged to Pastor Cohron. Shaw had come to him at midnight weeks before, stating his frustration with Ellwood. He even went so far as to tell Cohron, "I won't be coming to church anymore because I don't want to be a hypocrite." Not being able to help Ellwood was destroying him. Pastor Cohron promised, "I'll never stop fighting or praying for your soul.

There will be a pastor standing at the gates of hell to keep you from going in, Walt."

Carlson stood shaking. His gun was loaded, ready, but the children! How could he splatter Shaw across the stairwell in front of little kids? Thwarted, he arrested Shaw. Ellwood surrendered without resistance. A perpetual victim of egomania and loose lips, he, according to Detective Pete Mittleman's court testimony, bragged of his involvement in burglaries before he was ever questioned. "You've done it now officer Mittleman," Ellwood told Mittleman as the detective tried to read him his rights. "You have just arrested the best burglars in the state of Florida," Ellwood braggud.

Mittleman stated that Ellwood pointed to a black gym bag in the apartment and said, "There's something you should take with you." The detectives seized the bag, which contained all the articles required for a burglary – "gloves, ski-masks and various tools and guns," as reported by Lisa Conners of the *Jacksonville Times-Union* in an article entitled "Self-Described Top Burglar Convicted."

Shaw's arrest meant a parole violation. That, however, was the least of his problems. Ellwood had bragged "the best burglars in the state of Florida," meaning Shaw and himself. He had credited Shaw as his collaborator in a string of burglaries. The development was a hot news story. Shaw was described as a "master criminal."

The prosecutor assigned to the case was Mike Weatherby. *(Weatherby, in 1987, has represented defendant Carlos Lehder Rizas, the heavily publicized cocaine king from Colombia).* Weatherby offered Walter the choice of either facing burglary charges or pleading guilty to a parole violation. Weatherby promised that if Shaw went on trial for burglary and was found guilty by a jury, he would be behind bars for a minimum of thirty years, and with his record he would go full-term. Shaw's declaration of innocence did not impress Weatherby. He wanted Walter anyway he could get him.

Shaw decided not to gamble with another trial, especially since his financial status would have placed his defense in the hands of a court-appointed public defender. He was handed a four-year sentence for his second parole violation. With his case out of the way, he agreed to help Ellwood in his trial, even though Ellwood had cost him four years of his life. Ellwood's attorney concocted the story that Walter had forced Ellwood to burglarize. The court testimony, as reported by *Jacksonville Times-Union* staff writer Conners, "Ellwood told jurors that Shaw threatened to kill his sister and niece if he didn't come to Jacksonville from Miami last November. 'He said that if I didn't come to Jacksonville, I'd have my sister's head in an ice bucket when I returned,' Ellwood testified. Ellwood said Shaw beat him and told him repeatedly about his mob exploits" . . . "under cross-examination by Assistant State Attorney Edward Booth, the defendant testified, 'Did he (Shaw) put a gun to your head?' Booth asked Ellwood. 'No, he didn't have to,' Ellwood said, adding that Shaw's reputation for violence and organized crime connections were enough to convince him. Shaw, unshaved and wearing white prison garb, would not talk about the coercion. 'I take the Fifth Amendment on that,' Shaw said when asked if he had threatened Ellwood."

Before Shaw entered prison he thought of the price he had paid and would continue to pay for Christ's command to "love they neighbor as thyself." Taking the Fifth Amendment might as well have been lying, the way he saw it, and that *after* Ellwood had blamed him for ninety-eight burglaries. Just before taking the long ride to be processed for a long stint in prison, he met Weatherby, who displaying unusual pleasure, informed him that he had yielded to a bluff. The fact was, admitted Weatherby, that the case against him was weak and he doubtlessly would have been acquitted in court.

Walter wasn't even a good actor or liar anymore. The jury did not fall for his Fifth Amendment plea, nor did they believe his confession of beating Ellwood. Ellwood, still cocky, stood in court to hear the jury's decision – guilty as charged. The judge took little time to sentence him to forty years.

48

CHAPTER FORTY-EIGHT

The Avon Park Correctional Institute was Walter's home for the first eighteen months of his sentence. Pastor Cohron drove from Jacksonville three times a week. The trips took four hours each way. Walter believed that he had irrevocably separated himself from God. His actions were, in his mind, unforgivable. Cohron wouldn't let him destroy himself. He explained repeatedly, turning in the Bible to passage after passage, that God's forgiveness was always available, and that only in unrepentance, only in refusing to turn to God, did Walter forfeit forgiveness. Walter's drunkenness and involvement with Ellwood in court broke his fellowship, but it could be restored, completely restored, when Walter was willing to turn to the Lord. "Walter, it takes a lifetime to renew your mind. Believe me, you'll make many more mistakes and God will always be there to forgive you when you turn to him," Cohron assured him.

Walter finally admitted that "even in my worst depression and guilt, I could feel God still loved me." Later he would say that, "it was that love, God's love, that gave me the determination to keep going."

Out of respect for Pastor Cohron's dedication, prison officials allowed Walter to transfer to Lawtey Correctional Institute near Jacksonville. After the relocation, Pastor Cohron visited him daily, and at Cohron's suggestion, in 1983, Walter enrolled in Zoe Bible College, which offered divinity degrees to inmates. Behind bars, separated from all social contact, without a single friend other than Pastor Cohron, and after all the catastrophes that had occurred since his conversion, ironically, Walter finally laid hold of the peace necessary to free himself.

The *Gainesville Sun*, on Saturday, October 6, 1984, in an article entitled "Putting God Behind Bars," stated that "Chaplain Smith had pointed out Walter Shaw as a 'strong Christian.' Shaw told colleagues during his animated presentation that his father was incarcerated the day before. Shaw, who resembles in appearance actor Dustin Hoffman, talks fast with a hint of a Brooklyn accent, blending gangland phrases with gospel. 'I've done some really bad things in my life,' Shaw says. 'But God's been real good to me. God will bless you in your darkest hour . . . God's forgiven me for my past,' Shaw added. 'He took a big burden from me when he did that. God will get the glory.' "

One question still haunted Walter. What had happened to the $200,000 contract? Had it just disappeared? He knew better. In April of 1983, the mystery was solved. Earlier, in April of 1980, Shaw testified in a case involving Annello Della Croce who, according to the Associated Press, was "reputed underboss of the nation's largest Mafia organization for almost two decades. He was described by a federal judge as a top-level hoodlum, a danger to society, a menace to the community, a parasite who lives off the blood of honest people . . . A Manhattan assistant district attorney [said of him] 'the godfather of all crime in New York City.' New Jersey state police referred to Mr. Della Croce's proclivity toward violence and accused him of ordering the 1979 murder of Carmine Galante, the leader of the Bonanno crime organization."

It was the slaying of Galante that concerned Walter. A government informant, none other than Salerno, testified, according to Lloyd Brown of the *Jacksonville Times-Union* in an April 22, 1980, article that "he [Salerno] attended a meeting in a New York restaurant in 1974, where Annello Della Croce put out a hit on a Charles Calise. Della Croce is also a suspect in slaying top mobster Carmine Galante," Brown reported. "My source, convicted burglar Walter Thiel Shaw, also known as Archie Lewis, said Salerno could not have been at a meeting in New York because the two of them were busy breaking into houses. Shaw said, 'Salerno is a lyin' rat. He doesn't know anything about any meeting.' If information provided this column by a 'soldier' [Shaw] in the ranks of crime is correct, certain evidence presented in the current trial of a top mobster [Della Croce] may be of dubious credibility," Brown concluded.

Shaw had hoped that his testimony against Salerno, as well as the fact that Salerno had testified against Della Croce, would prove that he did not deserve the $200,000 contract. Rather, Salerno had been the informer all along.

In April of 1983, Shaw was subpoenaed to appear in Miami court where The Bear was facing an important battle. In a sworn affidavit Walter stated, "I was then transported to the United States Court House at Fort Lauderdale – now, at 9:55, or thereabouts, two FBI agents who said that's what they were came to take me upstairs to meet a man by the name of Mr. Luther R. Genge. The following conversation was held between me and Agent LaManna, and is true and accurate to the best of my knowledge and belief":

Shaw: "Why am I here?"

LaManna: "We want to ask some questions about some past associates of yours."

Shaw: "Does this have anything to do with The Bear".

LaManna: "Yes, he's going to trial and we want to get him."

Instead of helping LaManna and Federal Prosecutor Genge, Shaw burst their ploy wide open in court.

Berman, The Bear's attorney, asked Shaw on the witness stand, "Do you recall if he [Genge] used the words, 'We'll get him.'"

"Yes, he did say that," Walter replied. When he was cross-examined, Genge accused him of being an informant. Walter exploded and gave one of his greatest performances. "Could you come a little closer, Mr. Genge?" Walter requested.

Genge moved forward. Walter cleared his throat of mucus and spit right into his face. "Listen," he blasted loudly, "hell could freeze over and I wouldn't tell you nothing."

Escorted by two federal marshals, Shaw passed the defense table and said to The Bear, "I wish you the best." His efforts were effective. Salerno went into hiding under the marshal plan immediately. Walter's dramatic testimony, and his use of the face of a federal prosecutor for a spittoon were in the hearts and minds of his executioners, validation of his innocence. He returned to Lawtey to tell Pastor Cohron about his reunion with The Bear. Cohron admonished him for spitting on Genge, but assured him that Christ's work was lifelong.

Walter reflected on the court appearance. The Bear, the courtroom, the intrigue and high drama had lost their luster. His mailbox was stuffed with letters from believers in the Jacksonville area who had, in one way or another, heard of his faith and his recent challenges. These letters, mostly handwritten, were full of expressions of love and acceptance for him, a man they had never met. People like that, people who loved no matter what, people who didn't put out contracts or brutalize, people who were Christlike, true Christians, people such as Pastor Cohron, they were his friends now.

In December of 1985, Walter was out of prison on work-release again. He had just graduated from Zoe Bible College. And in April 1986 he was freed completely.

49

CHAPTER FOURTY-NINE

Annie Tique's is a bar in Jacksonville, Florida. In May of 1986, Walter received a call from Tony Stanfa, an old friend during his crime days. It was late, his friend was desperate. Pleading, he asked Walter to join him, to rescue him.

Walter arrived at 11:30 that night. He walked into the bar and sat down next to Stanfa. Stanfa was in shambles. He had tried to live right, he explained, but everything was going wrong. Walter understood him completely. He opened his mouth and words flowed out perfectly, better than any of his old cons. These words, however, were honest. Stanfa could tell because they were filled with pain, and finally, triumph. In the midnight darkness of the bar, with booze and jukebox blaring, Tony Stanfa had seen the light; he heard Walter's soft voice discussing God's forgiveness, love, and the opportunity to wipe the slate clean. Tony Stanfa committed – he would "stick it out." Inside, Walter was exhilarated, his young friend would make it.

Outside, as the two left the building, trouble started. The new convert's past caught him at a tender moment. With eyes still wet from tears, Stanfa found himself surrounded by old enemies. A fight broke out. Walter walked away. He had already learned that help can only be extended so far.

Suddenly, Walter heard a familiar "click." He froze. Silence. The men stopped shouting at each other. *Who had the gun?* Several seconds passed and Walter moved. He turned – turned into an explosion of flesh and blood, as brain tissue splattered across his chest. He looked up in horror. Tony was standing. Thank God, he was alive. Walter looked down at his shirt, nearly gagging, he hadn't seen that much blood since his suicide attempt. He hadn't seen shredded brain matter since...It was like a nightmare. Stuck in another freezeframe, he had been transported back in time. Back? – he could not go back. *God help me . . . I won't go back.*

There wasn't any time to figure out what happened. Tony lunged forward, grabbed Walter by the wrist, and frantically pulled him toward the car. Zombie-like, Walter dumped his body into the passenger's side. As the car sped down the road, he stared straight out the window. The blood, once warm, was becoming cold. *Have I done something wrong? Is this wrong? Have I ruined everything? What do I do? What do I do?*

"Stop! Stop the car!" Walter's cry pierced the timid silence. Stanfa slammed on the brakes. Walter, chest heaving, explained that he would not continue the journey unless the destination was a police station. Stanfa stared, eyes wide open. At last he made a U-turn and headed toward the police station.

The following December , a young man who had been a Christian just three weeks caught his wife in the act of adultery. He took a gun and shot himself. The bullet pierced his chest and caused his left lung to collapse. Doctors at the University Memorial Hospital, on West 8th Street in Jacksonville, did not expect him to live. A friend alerted several Jacksonville churches to the crisis. They had never heard of the young man.

He received no visitors, and his condition deteriorated.

Finally, the friend heard about an ex-con who was trying his hand at the ministry. Skeptical, the friend called Walter Shaw, even though she figured he was running a scam. That same day Walter arrived at the hospital. Before he entered the room he was warned: "Remember he can't talk, and he's in terrible pain. He'll probably die – he won't fight to live, but can you blame him – he's got nothing to live for."

Walter braced himself for the worst, but, at that, wasn't prepared for the sight. A tracheotomy had been performed, and tubes riddled the man's throat. Looking down at the patient, Walter said, "Blink if you can understand me." The man blinked his eyelids. "I want you to know that Jesus still loves you, my friend, there's nothing in the world you could ever do to make Him stop loving you. Do you wanna know how I know?" Walter pulled his sleeves back, revealing the scars on his wrists and hand. "See, I know right where you are, I tried to kill myself too . . ." The story continued for fifteen or twenty minutes. It ended with a prayer and this: "If God can forgive me, man, he can forgive *anybody*." Walter smiled. "Don't give up, God loves you," he said seriously, and "so do I."

The man tried to blink, but it was slow going. His eyelids were like fins pushing against the surface of a pool of water. But they connected, and several tears splashed over his eyelashes. From that day forward, he clawed for his existence. Today he is alive and well.

Walter Shaw, once suicidal himself, the consummate egotist, self-centered and cruel, made the difference. He received no money for the visit. Nor any awards. And, until now, no one has ever mentioned the incident. He went to the hospital that December night because he knew he could help, because he knew Christ could help.

Such profound change in an individual cannot be

categorized as rehabilitation. Studies show that for criminals like Walter Shaw who repeatedly commit crimes, attempts at rehabilitation are usually futile. Recidivists are too solidly entrenched in their ways to be successfully reached by psychologists and positive thinking. On the other hand, studies also show that increasing numbers of repeat offenders *are* being changed, and to ask those who are working successfully in this field is to redefine one's terms. They speak not of rehabilitation but of rebirth. It is ironic that in an age of such scientific optimism and theological pessimism the social worker is failing where the miracle worker is not. Jesus Christ, regardless of current wisdom, seems to be a reality for a growing number of prisoners and ex-prisoners, of whom Walter Shaw is one. This has been his unique story. A man who gloried in crime transformed into a forgiven and giving believer.

There are many stories of victory, but much of Walter's life is a grind. Between January and April of 1987 his phone was turned off twice. The electricity in his home was shut off twice. He was evicted from his apartment once. Several times during these months, he has humbly driven to the Circle of Love street ministry to receive free food. Many times he has traveled across the Southeast to speak in churches, and the "love gifts" often fail to cover transportation. Worse, pastors and congregations turn cold shoulders. Fellowship seems unavailable to Walter Shaw. "I could pull down $40,000 in one night," he stated. "What do I have to do to prove that I'm for real?"

Walter has learned and is learning that life consists of minute by minute decisions. Daily he must choose whether or not he will follow the Lord. And it must be said that from a realistic standpoint the whole thing seems as if it could very well be short-lived. If the bills keep piling up . . . if the pressure continues . . . if the cold shoulders become ever more frigid

... if the resentment and suspicions rise ... then how will he make it? How can he continue to make the right decisions?

Shaw, the man who has seen and done it all, who once purchased custom-tailored suits with the frequency that construction workers buy six-packs, who earlier had as his trade-marks alligator shoes, monogrammed shirts, elegant restaurants and exotic automobiles, who still receives calls in the night from old buddies suggesting a con that would have less legal risk than the physical risk which a riveter has as a ship-builder. His commitment to minister has not brought material prosperity, far from it. He passes the elegant restaurants, on the way to the "Circle of Love" to get food.

Undoubtedly, the glamour, glitz, and excitement of the old world beckon for him late at night. Surely he is living in a house of cards. Given a fire or windstorm and he will either burn up or blow away. No philosophy can overcome all that. No amount of dedication is likely to conquer those difficulties. No force of will could resist such temptation. Still, in spite of overwhelming odds, there is one way he can win. There is one hope.

That which changed his life can certainly sustain it. Love ... the love of God. Walter says, in all sincerity, that he is simply in love with Jesus Christ. In that love and only in that love can he prevail. The Apostle Paul, who called himself "chief of sinners", knew well what survival depended upon. His immortal words speak of love as the only secure foundation in a world of illusion and deceit. Walter's future depends on his commitment to love. Indeed, if *mankind* seeks a future, that future will only be found in love.

Even the best people fail. Unfortunately, man is not a very "good" creature, not consistently so anyway. Some claim to be waiting for evolution to do its work, or for an inevitable process of perfection. That is interesting speculation, but it does

Walter, nor anyone alive today, precious little good. Fortunately, there is a way. A way for Walter, for anyone, for everyone – *a way* for right now.

And yet I will show you *a way* that is better by far:
If I could speak the languages of men, of angels too,
And have no love,
I am only a rattling pan or a clashing cymbal.
If I should have the gift of prophecy,
And know all secret truths, and knowledge in its every form,
And have such perfect faith that I could move mountains,
But have no love, I am nothing.
If I should dole out everything I have for charity,
And give my body up to torture in mere boasting pride,
But have no love, I get from it no good at all.
Love is so patient and so kind;
Love never boils with jealousy;
It never boasts, is never puffed with pride;
It does not act with rudeness, or insist upon its rights;
It never gets provoked, it never harbors evil thoughts;
Is never glad when wrong is done,
But always glad when truth prevails;
It bears up under anything,
It exercises faith in everything,
It keeps up hope in everything,
It gives us power to endure in anything.
Love never fails.

I Corinthians Thirteen
Williams translation

Such love is difficult to attain and impossible to maintain. But when Walter loses his way and he will, when anyone loses their way, and everyone does, there is an answer. There is that figure in history, that shatterer of stereotypes and limitations – at once kind and angry, peaceful and violent, humble and proud, defenseless and all-powerful. Hear Him, as he claims again and again, for all eternity, undoubtedly the boldest assertion ever made :

I am the way . . .

May Christ be heard. Amen.

Walter being searched before entering a correctional institution, 1987.

Mug shot of Walter while in prison.

Walter talking to Robert Van Buskirk, author of *Tail Winds*, and "Murf the Surf" Murphy, 1987.

with his grandmother, "Nana"
Walter at five

Walter's father (Walter Sr.)
and his mother (Betty Lou). Last Photograph
of his mother before her death, 1987.

Walter with his wife Barbara, May, 1987

Walter's two children,
Shelly and Randy, in 1973.

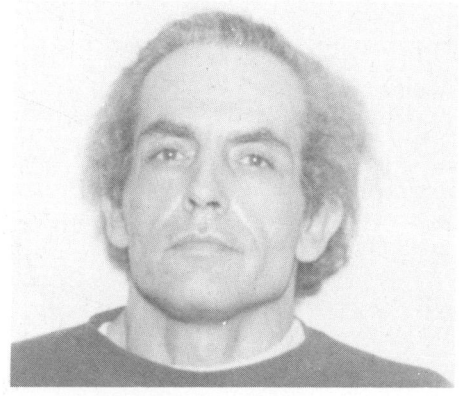

Peter Joseph Salerno, Walter's mentor in the "art" of burglary.

Walter and daughter Michele in 1972.

Walter speaking in Bill Glass Crusade, 1987.

Walter speaking at Lawtey Correctional Institute's chapel.

Walter talking to Robert Van Buskirk, author of *Tail Winds*.

Walter with Nicky Cruz, former New York gang member and the subject of the best-selling book *"The Cross and The Switch-blade."*

Walter with wife Barbara in 1987.

Pastor Wil Cohron and his wife Shirley.